Criminality and
Economic Conditions

1-617-227-0730

Criminality and
Economic Conditions

Willem Bonger

Abridged and with an Introduction by
AUSTIN T. TURK

INDIANA UNIVERSITY PRESS
Bloomington · London

Introduction Copyright © 1969
by Indiana University Press

All rights reserved

*No part of this book may be reproduced or utilized in any
form or by any means, electronic or mechanical, including
photocopying and recording, or by any information storage
and retrieval system, without permission in writing from
the publisher. The Association of American University
Presses' Resolution on Permissions constitutes the only
exception to this prohibition.*

*Published in Canada by Fitzhenry & Whiteside Limited,
Don Mills, Ontario, Canada*

Library of Congress catalog card number: 69-15992

Manufactured in the United States of America

Contents

PREFACE

A product of my belief that the original is better than an allusion in a textbook, this abridgement of Willem Bonger's famous treatise is intended primarily for classroom use in criminology and related courses. The student who wishes to read further is referred to the 1916 edition, published by Little, Brown and Company, of *Criminality and Economic Conditions*, since this small volume includes only Part II, Book II of that massive study. Moreover, the emphasis is upon Bonger's theoretical perspective rather than the details of his analysis, so tables, footnotes, and—for our purposes—extraneous textual material have been omitted. Editorial paraphrasing has been inserted when necessary for clarification or continuity, and such inserts are set off by brackets. Routine corrections of misspelling and other typographical errors in the 1916 edition have been made.

For their interest in this venture I am grateful to Richard Quinney, to my colleague Irving Zeitlin, and to Michael Aronson of the Indiana University Press. Critical readings of the introduction by Professors Quinney and Zeitlin were especially helpful. They cannot be blamed for what happened to their good advice on the way to the presses. Careful typists, like good wives, are valued "far above rubies." Among the select are Betty Beedie and Sandy Peterson.

Criminality and
Economic Conditions

AUSTIN T. TURK

Introduction

The Man and His Work[1]

Willem Adriaan Bonger was born in 1876 and died in 1940, choosing suicide rather than submission to the Nazi "scum." He received his doctorate from the University of Amsterdam in 1905, and subsequently achieved international eminence for his contributions to criminological knowledge. Major works available in English translation include *Criminality and Economic Conditions* (Boston: Little, Brown & Co., 1916), *An Introduction to Criminology* (London: Methuen & Co., Ltd., 1936), and *Race and Crime* (New York: Columbia University Press, 1943). In his life's work Bonger combined a passion to alleviate human misery with an equal passion for scientific knowledge. A dedicated but tough-minded socialist, he had contempt for both those who denigrated research as a basis for effective social action, and those who would use the search for knowledge as an excuse for a lack of personal commitment and involvement.

3

Contemporary Significance

Not long after its appearance in 1905, *Criminalité et conditions économiques* was selected by the newly organized American Institute of Criminal Law and Criminology to be translated and published as a volume in its distinguished "Modern Criminal Science Series." Accordingly, Henry Horton's translation was published, with Bonger himself assisting in the project by providing corrections to the French edition, footnote materials especially for the American edition, a critical reading of the translation—and a preface in which he was "fully convinced that my ideas about the etiology of crime will not be shared by a great many readers of the American edition." Indeed they were not; and by the end of the Depression, *Criminality and Economic Conditions* had become a minor classic, i.e., a book everyone knows about, a few have read, but hardly anyone ever uses. The trouble is, *Criminality* appears to have become a "classic" before its time.

Apart from distaste for his Marxist socialism, criminologists tended to give Bonger short shrift because of his preoccupation with relating criminality to the fundamentals of social order. As he noted, the attention of criminologists was focused upon explaining the deviant behavior of individuals; even sociological students of criminality would for decades to come be engrossed in demonstrating the superiority of their social psychologies over biologistic and narrowly psychologistic theories in accounting for such behavior. Sutherland, for instance, concentrated upon development of "differential association theory," deferring systematic treatment of the problem of "differential social organization"— i.e., the problem of explaining why people vary in exposure to criminogenic social experiences. Bonger, however, worked in the opposite direction—and against the currents of his time; he more or less assumed social learning as the key to understanding human behavior, and sought to explain how variations in social conditions determined variations in social learning, and therefore in behavior patterns. Thus, Bonger was read, acknowledged a scholar (albeit a radical fellow), and duly put aside when it came to getting on with the pressing business of research on criminal behavior.

Now that there is renewed interest in the bases of "law and order"—e.g., the recent organization and rapid expansion of the Law and Society Association—it is time to take Bonger's ideas seriously as having potential applicability to here-and-now theoretical and research issues. Obviously, his socialist theory of criminality—which in its essentials is accepted by a large proportion of the governments and people of the world—is not to be accepted or rejected on faith by criminologists. Our concern is solely to understand his theory, to divorce the really critical points from the errors of detail, and to determine the extent to which his explanation of criminality must be accepted, modified, supplemented, or rejected in favor of some superior alternative.

A Socialist Theory of Criminality

Underlying any explanation of criminality are assumptions regarding the predictability of human behavior and the nature of scientific inquiry. Bonger's position is that "the regularly and similarly-returning distribution of human inclinations and propensities is one of the postulates of criminal sociology; and, as a matter of fact, of the science of sociology as a whole."[2] Moreover, the scientist must assume that regularities do not just happen, but are determined by causal processes; "an indeterminist criminologist is a living *contradictio in adjecto*."[3] Undeniably man "*feels* free in his 'willing'—either wholly or partly," but with "a conceit only equalled by lack of logic, the conclusion is jumped at that causes do not, therefore, exist."[4] Yet, it does not follow—as some would have it—that determinism implies non-responsibility for one's actions; this is a dangerous and absurd notion. "On the contrary . . . determinism teaches us that every human being, without exception, is to be held accountable for his actions; not on the grounds of an imaginary free will, but because of the fact that he is a member of society, and that this society must take measures to protect itself."[5] Thus, the grounds of the individual's responsibility are to be found not in metaphysics, but in the fact of his involvement in social relations whose survival is contingent upon his conformity.

Returning to the assumption of causal determinism, whether that assumption can be demonstrated in practice is another issue. Though our data and analysis must be as exact as possible, and though we may move toward scientific laws, the "investigator in this field should . . . put out of his mind the illusion that this class of law can ever rank in dependability with, for instance, laws of nature"[6]—i.e., the laws established in the physical sciences. Philosophically, then, Bonger is a determinist; heuristically, he is a probabilist—which is, of course, characteristic of most working scientists today.

Bonger's philosopical foundations must be kept in mind if we are not to misconstrue his theory of criminality. As we shall see, the key propositions from his work constitute a determinist system of causal relationships. Nonetheless, Bonger himself never assumed that he or other "environmentalists" had validated beyond question and revision the theory which he was advancing.[7] He claimed only that his theory was on the right track, and clearly superior to the alternatives offered at that time in the literature of criminology. His intent was to present that theory as unambiguously as he could, along with the available evidence to which it was addressed. It is, therefore, an error to impute to Bonger—as van Bemmelen and others have done—a dogmatism impervious to soundly reasoned and empirically supported criticisms.[8] To be misled by the determinist *form* of its statement is to fail to understand the *substance* of Bonger's criminological theory—plainly offered as a *scientific* theory, ergo, one subject to confirmation, change, or rejection in the light of further theoretical and empirical work. With its claim to scientific standing having been established, Bonger's theory is developed as follows.

The task of explanation is to identify the motivation to commit criminal acts, to account for the fact that motivation is not always expressed in behavior, and to determine the sources of criminal motivation.[9] "The etiology of crime includes the three following problems:

First. Whence does the criminal thought in man arise?

Second. What forces are there in man which can prevent the execution of this criminal thought, and what is their origin?

Third. What is the occasion for the commission of criminal acts?" The first and third problems are not necessarily separable, since "the occasion may be one of the causes of the criminal thought." As the evidence makes it "certain that man is born with social instincts" capable—given "a favorable environment" —of preventing "egoistic thoughts from leading to egoistic acts," the crucial etiological question regarding *crime in general* is whether or not a given environment is in fact "favorable." Thus, one must determine the relationships among social conditions, egoism-altruism, and criminality. Given the general problem, however, it must be recognized that heredity may be relevant to a greater or lesser degree in the analysis of particular classes of criminal acts; and it must be recognized that the identification of persons as criminals is more or less influenced by the distribution of political-legal power. These general considerations are spelled out in the following propositions.[10]

1. "The abnormal element in crime is a social, not a biological, element. With the exception of a few special cases, crime lies within the boundaries of normal psychology and physiology. Such is the basic principle of criminal sociology." (*Intro.*, 75-76)

2. The response to crime is punishment—which is the deliberate application of penalties considered to be more severe than spontaneous "moral disapprobation"—administered in the name

of the community by its rulers, i.e., the state. (*Intro.*, 4-5; *Criminality*, 378)

3. "Crime belongs to the category of immoral actions." However, "one cannot speak of any action as being either immoral or criminal per se; there is, in fact, no such thing as a 'natural' offense." Immoral actions are antisocial acts "felt as such." (*Intro.*, 1-3) "Since the social structure is changing continually, the ideas of what is immoral (and consequently of what is or is not criminal) change with these modifications." (*Criminality*, 379) Great changes in conceptions of morality are reflected in criminal law. Nevertheless, "the tension between a rapidly-changing morality [as in the increasing displacement of bourgeois by socialist morality] and a comparatively static [predominantly bourgeois] criminal law can, at times, become very great." An important supplemental point is that it is a bad sign if criminality and immorality are coterminous, for "any society which threatens with punishment almost every transgression is internally weak." (*Intro.*, 3)

4. More specifically, crimes are "antisocial" acts, "harmful in a considerable degree to the interests . . . of those who have the power at their command." (*Criminality*, 379) [It should be noted that Bonger is not always clear in regard to the distinctions (a) between crimes as *actually harmful* and crimes as *perceived to be harmful*, and (b) between the interests of the body politic, i.e., the entire community, and those of the ruling class of the community. In particular, he appears to have moved somewhat away from the relative clarity of his views in *Criminality* toward a more moralistic and less analytical statement in his *Introduction*. Contrast, for instance the above propositions with these:

"Crime is a harmful social disease, with economic and moral costs to the body politic, as well as damage and grief to its victims and suffering for virtually all its agents." (*Intro.*, 5-6)

The moral are more important than the economic costs of crime, since "if criminality is closely bound up with the moral standards of a people, in return it sends out demoralizing influences towards the normal sections of the population." (*Intro.*, 6)

Since *Criminality* was addressed to his professional peers, while the *Introduction* was a textbook for beginning students, we take as Bonger's most considered statements the propositions found in the earlier rather than the later book, whenever we must choose between these sources.]

5. Thus, in "every society which is divided into a ruling class and a class ruled, penal law has been principally constituted according to the will of the former," even though criminal laws—probably most of them—may in fact be "directed against acts that are prejudicial to the interests of both classes equally." However, "hardly any act is punished if it does not injure the interests of the dominant class. . . . The rare exceptions are explained by the fact that the lower classes are not wholly without power." (*Criminality*, 379 80)

6. The ruling and ruled "groups into which the population of capitalistic countries is divided do not originate in the circumstances that men differ in their innate capacities, but in the system of production that is in force." (*Criminality*, 290)

7. The capitalist system, characterized by unrestrained competition, is necessarily held together by force rather than consensus. "The state is not an institution for the public well-being; it is chiefly a means of maintaining the external order in the disorder which results from the complicated and muddled system of capitalistic production; it is before all a system of police." (*Criminality*, 309) Needless to say, the order is one in which the interests of the capitalists are generally maintained even at the expense of the population as a whole.

8. Where, as under capitalism, relations are based upon exploitive exchange and force instead of cooperation and trust, there is "great uncertainty of existence" for all men, bourgeoisie as well as proletariat. (*Criminality*, 98)

9. Since (a) "the desire for pleasure is innate in every man"

and (b) "in our present society one can enjoy [all that is truly beautiful, all that nature, art, and science can offer man] only with plenty of money," men are encouraged in capitalist society to use any available means to obtain pleasure in general and money in particular. (*Criminality*, 362-63) Thus, "the present environment exercises an egoistic influence upon all men," while "compassion for the misfortunes of others inevitably becomes blunted, and a great part of morality . . . disappears." (*Criminality*, 532-33) In short, "as a consequence of the present environment, man has become very egoistic and hence more *capable of crime* than if the environment had developed the germs of altruism." (*Criminality*, 402)

10. If the environment makes both bourgeoisie and proletariat egoistic and therefore capable of crime, why then are the bourgeoisie less likely—as indicated by criminal statistics—than the proletariat to become criminals? The answer lies in the discriminatory nature of the legal system, which tends to legalize the egoistic actions of the bourgeoisie and to penalize those of the proletariat. "For example, a man who is enriched by the exploitation of children [child labor] may nevertheless remain all his life an honest man from the legal point of view. He does not think of stealing, because he has a surer and more lucrative means of getting wealth, although he lacks the moral sense which would prevent him from committing a crime if the thought of it occurred to him." (*Criminality*, 402)

11. As to those of the bourgeoisie who do commit crimes, their behavior is attributable to the conjunction of (a) an opportunity to gain an illegal advantage, with (b) their lack of moral sense. "It is generally believed that nothing is wanting in the moral education of one who has not known poverty, and has not been neglected; but this is a mistake. There can be no doubt that one of the factors of criminality among the bourgeoisie is bad education [in which the egoistic drive toward success at any price is inculcated]." (*Criminality*, 484)

12. Much crime is, of course, due to poverty. The relationship is, however, both direct (as in theft out of desperate need) and indirect: "poverty (taken in the sense of absolute want) kills the social sentiments in man, destroys in fact all relations beween men." (*Criminality*, 436) In any event, "it is not the total amount of wealth but [the manner of] its distribution that bears [most importantly] upon criminality." (*Criminality*, 91) The potency of economic want as a factor in crime causation is mainly determined by whether or not poverty is experienced as relative deprivation, in a social context (capitalism) wherein people are taught to equate economic advantage with intrinsic superiority and disadvantage with inferiority.

13. The environment may either aggravate or ease the adaptation problems of individuals with defective genetic endowments. "There are persons who are born with psychic defects. These persons adapt themselves to their environment only with difficulty [under the best of conditions; unfortunately such persons] have a smaller chance than others to succeed in our present society, where the fundamental principle is the warfare of all against all. Hence they are more likely to seek for means that others do not employ (prostitution, for example)." (*Criminality*, 354)

14. Finally, almost all crime will disappear as society progresses from competitive capitalism, through monopoly capitalism, to "having the means of production held in common," and ultimately to "a redistribution of property according to the maxim, 'to each according to his needs,' something that will probably be realized, but not in the immediate future." Short of this ultimate attainment, a residue of crime will persist; even then, there "will be crimes committed by pathological individuals, but this will come rather within the sphere of the physician. than that of the judge. And then we may even reach a state where these cases will decrease in large measure, since the social causes of degeneracy will disappear, and procreation by de-

generates be checked through the increased knowledge of the laws of heredity and the increasing sense of moral responsibility." (*Criminality*, 669-72)

To summarize, Bonger's theory is that, with reference to the amount of criminal behavior in a given population,

1. Egoism implies the capability of committing criminal acts, while altruism implies the absence of this capability (in regard to virtually all crimes).

2. Capitalism promotes egosim, and therefore the capability of committing crime; socialism promotes altruism, and therefore the absence of this capability.

3. The proneness to commit crime actually results in criminal behavior if

a. the egoistic person perceives an opportunity to gain by illegal action an advantage at the expense of others, and/or

b. opportunities to achieve gratification legally are denied, i.e., the legal system is biased.

4. Capitalism is characterized by both (3a) and (3b), while socialism will ultimately remove both the need and the opportunity to seek gratification at the expense of others. Consequently,

5. Capitalism causes crime; socialism will ultimately eliminate crime.

Evaluation

We may begin by distinguishing between the issues of (a) the cogency of Bonger's analysis of criminality in relation to the characteristics of nineteenth century capitalism, and (b) the validity of his analysis as a general theory of criminality. Few serious scholars will quarrel with his description of conditions found in the era of rugged capitalism; furthermore, his tracing of connections between those conditions and what was known of crime during that period makes eminent good sense, given the measures and conceptual tools then available. However, when we take up the second issue—and for present purposes the more crucial one—some major difficulties are encountered.

One fundamental defect in Bonger's theory is that pointed out by Kelsen and Stone, among many others, with respect to Marxian legal theory in general: the inability to resolve theoretically, rather than by fiat, the discrepancy between (a) the classic Marxist *definition* of the state as a pre-socialist instrument of class oppression, and (b) the recognition that—short of the perfection of a fully socialist society comprised of no one but completely altruistic people—pathological behavior must somehow be controlled.[11] Instead of providing a solution to the problem of relating political-legal processes to the issues of defining and controlling criminality, the Bonger theory finally avoids the problem by relegating both terms—"political-legal processes" and "criminality"—to the observed "capitalist" set of phenomena and eliminating them from some hypothetical "socialist" set of phenomena. Thus, there is to be no coercive structure of control because there can be no need for it in socialist society; yet, "pathological" individuals will appear, and the society must somehow be protected.

An attempted solution is implied in the statements that pathological deviant acts "will come rather within the sphere of the physician than that of the judge," although the incidence of such cases will be reduced to a minimum through "the increased knowledge of the laws of heredity and the increasing sense of moral responsibility" (proposition 14 above). Envisioned is the medical treatment of individuals whose physical degeneracy is too great to be neutralized by the most favorable environment, along with genetic engineering to prevent such persons from coming into existence. However, the unanswered question is, *who* shall decide what is to be done to whom? And if pathological individuals lack, by definition, sufficient moral sense to restrain themselves and to submit themselves for treatment, whose job will it be to restrain them for treatment? Certainly these questions have to be answered for a socialist as for any other form of society; and just as certainly it is not enough merely to exchange one set of decision-makers for another, calling one set—police, judges, wardens—"state" and the other—therapists, physicians, scientists—"no state." Such semantic changes may or may not correspond to any significant changes in the control structure; indeed the evidence indicates that whatever changes occur are likely to be in the direction of a more thorough (though perhaps "benevolent") despotism.[12]

Succinctly put, the point is that Bonger's thought founders largely because he was unable to escape the confines of his Marxism, i.e., to see that the political, conflict processes through which definitions of deviance (criminality) are created and enforced are not peculiar to "capitalist" societies, but are generic to social life.[13]

Given that the Bonger theory is deficient because it lacks a defensible sociology of law and social control, how promising is it as a social structural theory of deviant (criminal) behavior? The general thesis is that such behavior is almost entirely attributable to the combination of egoism and an environment in which opportunities are not equitably distributed. Therefore, the theory must be examined with respect to the adequacy of (a) the posited relationship between egoism-altruism and deviant behavior, (b) the conceptualization of "inequitable distribution of opportunities," and (c) the linking of (a) with (b).

Even if it is granted that some behavior is attributable primarily to biological rather than social psychological factors, it does not follow that all other behavior is caused by either egoism or altruism. Nor does it necessarily follow that deviant behavior is the acting out of egoistic impulses while socially acceptable behavior expresses altruistic impulses. Of course, Bonger does not pretend that his framework constitutes a theory of human motivation; his aim is to indicate, in "ideal typical" form, how certain cultural themes are related through social learning to broad categories of behavior. Nevertheless, in the absence of egoism-altruism measures and of a more explicit recognition of the complexity of motivation, his scheme easily leads one to impute egoism to those whose behavior is considered reprehensible (capitalists, criminals) and altruism to those whose behavior is deemed commendable (socialists, morally sensible people). An additional weakness in the egoism → deviant behavior formula is that it ignores the facts that ostensibly egoistic behavior may redound to the benefit of some collectivity and that self-sacrificing behavior in behalf of one part of a collectivity may injure the interests of another part. Further, it can be argued that deviant acts themselves perform such functions as defining the boundaries of the acceptable and unifying the collectivity against the threat.[14] Perhaps a paraphrase of Cohen's conclusion regarding the utility of "frustration-aggression" explanations of deviant behavior is the most generous assessment of Bonger's "egoism" explanation:

There is enough evidence in favor of the [egoism] hypothesis to persuade us that things often happen in the way it describes, but there are enough intractible data to convince us that it is not tenable as a general theory.[15]

What constitutes an "inequitable distribution of opportunities?" Bonger accepts the Marxian postulate than any distribution is inequitable which falls short of the formula "from each according to his abilitiy, to each according to his need." At the same time, however, he conceptualizes inequitable opportunity structure in terms of whether persons socialized to be egoistic in a capitalist environment are in fact able to compete as equals, to start at the same mark at the beginning of the footrace. Therefore, a fine distinction is suggested between (a) the characterization of a social structure as inherently inequitable, and (b) the characterization of the channels of opportunity within a given social structure as inequitable. That is, the system may itself be fundamentally inequitable, or else opportunities to succeed within the system may be available to some but not to others.

To Bonger the point would be academic, since his line of argument is that the freedom to compete in a capitalist system is not equally available *because* the system is intrinsically unjust. His problem is not that of extending "equal opportunity" to all within capitalist structure (an impossible task in the eyes of a Marxist), but that of replacing—by peaceful means as far as possible—capitalist with socialist structure.[16] The question is, assuming that the capitalist system is indeed inequitable, why should one expect the socialist system to be equitable?

In somewhat more concrete terms than those above, Bonger's answer is that socialist structure will be equitable because each will be given what he needs to contribute to the general welfare. This criterion assumes that the recipient will be altruistic, willing to do what he can to use his opportunities to benefit the collectivity as a whole. In its philosophical purity the criterion further assumes that each person will understand *how* he is to act for the common good, and assumes that all such altruistic acts will somehow coalesce into a mutually beneficial cooperative enterprise. Coercion will be unnecessary, and apparently so will direction and coordination—at least when a fully socialist society is achieved.

As appealing as this utopian vision may be, it is quite incompatible with what is so far known of human behavior and social processes. Without attempting formal citations, we may simply confront the vision with the following observations.

First, although there are grounds for expecting that more socially sensitive personalities can be produced, there is ample evidence that human beings cannot be expected to be as utterly selfless as Bonger's "socialist man" is supposed to be.[17] It is by now a truism that each person is unique, since each has emerged through a unique combination of biological capacities and socializing experiences. Individuality, in turn, implies the continuing potential, even inevitability, of both conforming (altruistic?)

and deviant (egoistic?) behavior—as was long ago pointed out by Durkheim.

Second, neither the capitalist nor the socialist version of the "unseen hand" is tenable in light of the phenomenon of leadership role differentiation, which is found in social entities from the smallest, least specialized and ephemeral to the largest, most specialized and durable. In every collectivity the membership tends in time to be differentiated into leaders (coordinators, influentials, authorities) and followers (operatives, assenters, subjects). The operations of the system then turn out to be in large part functions of the decisions and performances of leaders and followers in interaction with one another. Whatever else is true of social structures, it is clear that they do not somehow run themselves.

Third, while the problem of material scarcity may well be eliminated in future through the application of scientific knowledge to economic processes, it is plain that men require not only tangible but also intangible resources—e.g., status, for which human beings seem to have an insatiable appetite. Moreover, the tendency of men to associate status with control (not necessarily ownership, or even consumption) of material resources makes the problem of material resources far more complex than that of abolishing material scarcity. How can status and control be allocated according to the simple notion of "need," since both are defined relative to someone else's having less? Who is to draw the line between what men want and what they need?

Fourth, given the facts of individuality, of leadership role differentiation, and of differential status and control, one cannot expect that the justice of social arrangements—whatever they may be—will always be apparent to everyone concerned. Sooner or later someone asks why a thing should be, and someone answers that it need not be. The inevitable differences in perception and evaluation can never be removed once and forever, but pose a constant threat to any given order. As challenges appear, the relative validity of "conservative" and "radical" views is determined by the outcomes of conflicts—which may take any form from argument and debate to war. Thus, the problems of dissensus, deviance, and control are never finally solved; the obvious corollary is, as Dahrendorf has put it, that justice is "rather than an unchanging, real or imagined state of affairs, the permanently changing outcome of the dialectics of power and resistance."[18]

In summary, the Bonger theory cannot stand as a general theory of either (a) criminality in relation to legal power, or (b) deviant behavior in relation to social structure. It begs the question of power, and fails to provide a plausible alternative to the set of social conditions presumed to cause deviant behavior. Nevertheless, much of Bonger's analysis of specific social conditions in relation to particular forms of deviant behavior, and of connections between legal processes and social conflicts in the world which he knew, is still viable—as a source of theoretical insights and of hypotheses for empirical research. Possibly his greatest contribution may turn out to be his insistence that criminologists must consider not only *direct* relations between economic variables and criminality, but also the *indirect* relations as economic effects are mediated through the other elements of social structure.

Notes

1. For a heavily psychoanalytic and critical treatment of Bonger and his work, see J. M. van Bemmelen's paper reprinted in *Pioneers in Criminology*, ed. Hermann Mannheim (Chicago: Quadrangle Books, Inc., 1960), pp. 349-63. Bonger himself might well have dismissed most of van Bemmelen's remarks as irrelevant nonsense.

2. *An Introduction to Criminology*, tr. Emil van Loo (London: Methuen & Co., Ltd., 1936), p. 121.

3. Ibid., p. 20.

4. Ibid., pp. 21-22.

5. Ibid., p. 23. Bonger was never clear on when the individual was justified in rebelling against "society"; even his discussion of political crime appears to reflect a basic conservatism difficult to reconcile with his Marxism.

6. Ibid., p. 20.

7. Regarding the "economic environmentalists," although they "have focused attention in a precise manner on one definite aspect of the *Théorie du milieu*, which had remained rather vague in the hands of the French authors, . . . it cannot be maintained that they have succeeded in proving their thesis; they have made it acceptable, no more." (Ibid., p. 83.)

8. With respect to his scientific work, as apart from his political convictions and actions, Bonger was no more a "dogmatic Marxist" than was Karl Marx himself. A presentation and assessment of "nondogmatic Marxism" is Irving C. Zeitlin's *Marxism: A Re-Examination* (Princeton, N.J.: D. VanNostrand Co., Inc., 1967).

9. The quotes in the remainder of this paragraph are from *Criminality and Economic Conditions*, tr. Henry P. Horton (Boston: Little, Brown & Co., 1916), pp. 401-402.

10. Hereafter, page references to the two Bonger books cited above will be informal (e.g., *Intro.*, 121; *Criminality*, 379) and inserted where appropriate in the text.

11. Hans Kelsen, *The Communist Theory of Law* (New York: Frederick A. Praeger, Inc., 1955); Julius Stone, *Social Dimensions of Law and Justice* (Stanford, Calif.: Stanford University Press, 1966), pp. 490-515.

12. Austin T. Turk, "Psychiatry vs. the Law—Therefore?" *Criminologica*, 5 (November, 1967), pp. 30-35.

13. On the general point, see Richard Quinney, "Crime in Political Perspective," *The American Behavioral Scientist*, 8 (December, 1964), pp. 19-22. For an effort to begin constructing a criminological theory in which the pervasiveness of social conflict is explicitly recognized, see Austin T. Turk, "Conflict and Criminality," *American Sociological Review*, 31 (June, 1966), pp. 338-52.

14. Albert K. Cohen, *Deviance and Control* (Englewood Cliffs, N.J.: Prentice-Hall, Inc., 1966), pp. 6-11.

15. Ibid., p. 62.

16. Within criminological theory the leading "bourgeois" alternative to such a radical critique of capitalism is, of course, anomie theory as developed by Merton, Cloward, and Ohlin, and others. (For crit-

ical summaries of this literature, along with an extensive bibliography, see Marshall B. Clinard, ed., *Anomie and Deviant Behavior*, New York: The Free Press of Glencoe, 1964.) While Bonger's theory finds the only solution in *replacing* the capitalist system, anomie "opportunity structure" theory offers the hope of *changing* the system, by eliminating the—in principle—artificial handicaps (e.g., racial discrimination, cultural deprivation, ignorance of legal rights and inability to assert them) preventing fair competition in the struggle for success, the universal goal, and therefore producing frustration, disillusionment, and deviant behavior. Whether one's preference be the one perspective or the other, it is still too soon in the effort to alleviate the crime problem by warring on poverty for anyone to be able to determine the extent to which the problem can, or cannot, be handled by structural changes short of radical transformation of the system.

17. Marx himself did not picture socialist man as such an automaton; rather, individuality would be fully realized in a socially sensitive person who—freed of the excessive constraints of life in a pre-socialist environment—would be able "to hunt in the morning, fish in the afternoon, rear cattle in the evening, criticize after dinner, just [as he wished], without ever [being forced into the narrow mold of] hunter, fisherman, shepherd or critic." Karl Marx and Frederick Engels, *The German Ideology* (New York: International Publishers Edition, 1947), p. 22.

18. Ralf Dahrendorf, *In Praise of Thrasymachus* (Eugene, Ore.: University of Oregon, The Henry Failing Distinguished Lecture, April 25, 1966), p. 31.

I
General Considerations

A. Definition of Crime

Crime belongs to the category of punishable acts. However, as the term is applicable to only a part of such acts, it is necessary to be more exact. The best way to do this, in my opinion, is to exclude successively all the groups of acts which are punishable without being crimes.

The first exclusion is in connection with the question, "Who is it that punishes?" You cannot call that a crime against which one or several individuals take action of their own motion, and where the social group to which they belong does not move as such. In this case the word "punish" is an improper term, for the act in question is one of personal vengeance. Nor can you apply the name of crime to the act of a group of persons forming a social entity, against an analogous group. The reaction of the second group called forth by such act is not properly punishment, but "blood-" or "group-vengeance," and is in reality nothing but a kind of war.

The second exclusion concerns the nature of the punishment. Acts which bring no other punishment than moral disapprobation are not reckoned as crimes. They are not so called unless they are threatened with something more severe than this.

The provisional result is, then, as follows: A crime is an act committed within a group of persons that form a social unit, and whose author is punished by the group (or a part of it) as such, or by organs designated for this purpose, and this by a penalty whose nature is considered to be more severe than that of moral disapprobation. This definition, however, considers only the formal side of the conception of crime; it says nothing as to its essence. It is proper, then, to consider next the material side.

Crime is an act. The question which presents itself first of all is this: Is crime considered from a biological point of view an abnormal act? The answer to this, which is of the highest importance for the etiology of crime, must be negative. From a biological point of view almost all crimes must be ranked as normal acts. The process which takes place in the brain of the gendarme when he kills a poacher who resists arrest is identical with that which takes place in the brain of the poacher killing the gendarme who pursues him. It is only the social environment which classes the second act rather than the first as a crime. From the biological point of view homicide is not an abnormal act. Sociology and history prove that men have always killed when they thought it necessary. No one would maintain, for example, that those who take part in a war are biologically abnormal.

The same observation may be applied to assaults. No anthropologist would maintain that a policeman clubbing a mob of strikers was performing a biologically abnormal act, or that the strikers were abnormal because they did not choose to let themselves be maltreated without defending themselves. It is only the social circumstances which class this defense as a crime, and cause the action of the policeman to be considered otherwise.

The same thing is true with regard to theft. For centuries it was considered the right of the soldiers to pillage the country of the conquered (and in colonial wars it is still done at times). Soldiers are not, however, from this fact considered to be biologically abnormal individuals. And yet there is no biological difference between these acts and those of the ordinary thief; for anthropology does not ask whether one steals on a large scale or on a small.

Continuing our researches into the essence of crime, it is obvious that it is an immoral act, and one of a serious character. Why do we find any act immoral? This question cannot be answered by asking of each individual separately, Why do you think such and such an act immoral? Moral disapprobation is primarily a question of feeling; ordinarily we take no account of why any given act is approved or disapproved by us. Sociology alone can solve the problem by taking the acts considered as immoral in relation with the social organization in which they take place. And in treating the matter thus we observe that the acts called immoral are those which are harmful to the interests of a group of persons united by the same interests. Since the social structure is changing continually, the ideas of what is immoral (and consequently of what is or is not criminal) change with these modifications.

Considered in this way from the material side, a crime is an anti-social act, an act which is harmful in a considerable degree to the interests of a certain group of persons. This definition is not yet complete, however, for many acts of this nature are not crimes.

The best thing to do in order to find what is lacking in this definition is to examine a concrete case. A short time ago there was added to the Dutch penal code a new article threatening with a penal term of some years the railroad employe who went out on a strike. The proposal of this law, presented after a partial strike of the railroad employes, aroused great indignation on the part of organized labor, while the bourgeoisie in general regarded a strike as an immoral act which would henceforth be followed by a severe penalty. Notwithstanding the violent opposition on the part of the deputies of the labor party the plan was accepted.

It is clear that what must be added to our definition (already contained implicitly in the formal definition) is that the act must be prejudicial to the interests of those who have the power at their command. If, in the case cited above, the deputies of the proletariat had had the majority the Dutch penal code would contain no penalties against railroad employes on a strike. Power then is the necessary condition for those who wish to class a certain act as a crime.

It follows that in every society which is divided into a ruling class and a class ruled penal law has been principally constituted according to the will of the former. We must at once add that the present legal prescriptions are not always directed against the class of those ruled, but that most of them are directed against acts that are prejudicial to the interests of both classes equally (for example, homicide, rape, etc.). These acts would without doubt continue to be considered criminal if the power were to pass into the hands of those who are at present the governed. However, in every existing penal code hardly any act is punished if it does not injure the interests of the dominant class as well as the other, and if the law touching it protects only the interests of the class dominated. The rare exceptions are explained by the fact that the lower classes are not wholly without power.

Before closing our observations we must put the question, What is the object of punishment? It seems to me that there are elements of different nature in punishment as prescribed in our present penal codes. To begin with the object of punishment is to be found in the feelings of vengeance excited by the crime, for which satisfaction is desired. But after this punishment has three things in view:

First, To put the criminal where he can do no further harm, either permanently or for a certain period.

Second, To inspire the criminal, and other persons as well, with a fear of committing crime.

Third, To reform the criminal as far as possible.

Most criminologists do not admit that punishment is still in great part a manifestation of the desire for vengeance (although regulated). Nevertheless it is indubitable that he who desires that some one shall be punished solely because he has committed a misdeed, and without his punishment's being of any use to the criminal or to others, wishes simply to satisfy his feelings of revenge. The most subtle theories cannot refute this fact. Those who from the height of their knowledge disdain the primitive peoples who practice the rule of "eye for eye, tooth for tooth," are nevertheless on the same plane in this matter, as those they scorn.

It is unnecessary to say that the minority that wishes to exclude all idea of vengeance from the penal code, and sees in it only a means of securing the safety of society, and, if possible, of reforming the criminal, is at present still very small, so that the ideas of this group are almost never realized in our present penalties.

This is our conclusion, then, that a crime is an act committed within a group of persons forming a social unit; that it prejudices the interests of all, or of those of the group who are powerful; that, for this reason, the author of the crime is punished by the group (or a part of the group) as such or by specially ordained instruments, and this by a penalty more severe than moral disapprobation.

To find the causes of crime we must, then, first solve the question: "Why does an individual do acts injurious to the interests of those with whom he forms a social unit?," or in other words: "Why does a man act egoistically?"

B. The Origin of Egoistic Acts in General

What are the causes of egoistic acts? How does it happen that one man does harm to another? The answers that have been given to this primeval question may be divided into two groups. The first group attributes the cause to the man himself, the second to his environment.

The great majority of persons who treat of this question settle it in favor of innate egoism. They are of the opinion that man is egoistic by nature and that environment can produce no change in this (this is implied in the Christian doctrine of original sin). This opinion, in order to be accepted as true, needs facts to prove that egoism has always and everywhere been the same among men.

Others, among whom are most of the well-known sociologists, also consider egoism as a fundamental trait of man, but are at the same time of the opinion that little by little egoism has decreased, that altruism has developed, and that this process continues. For this hypothesis to be correct it must be shown by the facts:

First. That the peoples of a much lower degree of social evolution than ours show much more egoistic traits of character.

Second. That the animals from whom man has descended are inveterate egoists.

This theory is naturally of the highest importance for criminal science, and it becomes still more so from the fact that, according to Professor Lombroso, crime is a manifestation of atavism, that is, that some individuals present anew traits of character belonging to their very remote ancestors. The criminal would thus be a savage in our present society. We must therefore examine to see whether the said theory is correct.

❖   ❖   ❖

I am of the opinion that no one, taking the above facts into consideration, will maintain that man has always and everywhere shown the same egoistic traits, or that there has been a gradual evolution from egoism towards altruism.

It would be a mistake, however, to suppose that primitive peoples present under all circumstances the altruistic characteristics that I have mentioned. I have already remarked that the position of woman is in general very dependent. In general the primitive peoples are very fond of their children and give them very tender care. Nevertheless infanticide is not uncommon among those who are at a low stage of civilization. And I have already remarked that among nomadic peoples the sick and aged were often abandoned. Here are then, contradictions which it is necessary to explain.

Apparently—but only apparently—an evolution from egoism towards altruism has really taken place and has not yet ceased. This appearance is the effect of the alteration in the character of the egoism under the present economic system; it has become less *violent* than at earlier periods. The fight is no longer carried on with fire-arms or cold steel, but with other weapons no less dangerous, and this is what is generally lost sight of. We note that in ancient times the prisoners were killed; that later they were sold into slavery; that slavery was superseded by serfdom, which in its turn gave place to free labor.

But it is not always a growing altruistic sentiment that has been the motive in these changes. The life of prisoners of war has not been spared from reasons of humanity, but because the extension of the productivity of labor made it more profitable to make a prisoner work than to kill him. And slavery was not abolished because slave-owners had become less egoistic, but because it was more profitable to make free laborers work than to make slaves do so. We cannot speak of the diminution of egoism, but of the moderating of violence in the course of time. It cannot be maintained that a capitalist who tried by a lock-out to force his workmen to break with their union, in order that he may escape the danger of a decrease in his profits through a strike, and who in this way condemns them and their families to hunger, is less egoistic than the slave-owner driving his slaves to harder labor. The former does not use force—it is useless—he has a surer weapon at his command, the suffering with which he can strike his workmen; he *seems* less egoistic, but in reality is as egoistic as the latter. The great speculator who, by manipulating the market, forces thousands of persons to pay more for the necessaries of life, and to become his tributaries as it were, is not less egoistic than the robber-baron of the middle ages who, arms in hand, forced the traveling merchants to pay him tribute. The difference is merely that the former attains his end without using violence like the latter. Capitalism is a system of exploitation in which, in place of the exploited person's being robbed he is compelled by poverty to use all his powers for the benefit of the exploiter.

The same thing is true of colonial history. At first the aborigines of the countries explored by the Europeans were often pillaged and massacred. This system has long been abandoned, not from altruism however, but because it is more profitable to make a conquered people work than to pillage and exterminate them. When they do not submit voluntarily, force is used as heretofore.

The apparent improvement has yet another cause. Christianity preaches "Thou shalt love thy neighbor as thy self." And since this maxim has been often preached and many Christians have it always in their mouths, men come to believe that it is really put into practice. The contrary is true. The fact that the duty of altruism is so much insisted upon is the *most convincing proof that it is not generally practiced* or it would not be so much spoken and preached about. There are many persons in our days who ask nothing better than to see men act altruistically, but they preach in the wilderness; their wish has not come true. Present society is moulded by egoism. The egoism is less violent, however, and more disguised.

Before speaking of the real causes of egoism and altruism it may be well to attempt to answer the question," Whence come these inexact ideas?" It is not difficult, in my opinion, to explain how it comes about that many men believe that the "homo homini lupus" of Hobbes has been true always and everywhere. The adherents of this opinion have studied principally men who live under capitalism, or under civilization; their correct conclusion has been that egoism is the predominant characteristic of these men, and they have adopted the simplest explanation of the phenomenon and say that this trait is inborn.

If they had known the periods anterior to civilization, they would have noted that the "homo homini lupus" is an historical phenomenon applicable during a relatively short period, and that consequently it is impossible that egoism should be innate in man. However great have been the social modifications during the period of civilization, the principal aim of men has always been, and still is, to acquire personal wealth, and men still remain divided into classes, that is into groups whose economic interests are contrary. This is why an examination of the earlier periods is of such high importance for sociology.

An erroneous interpretation of the Darwinian theory has also contributed to bring about the strange notion of the eternal character of the struggle of all against all. Darwin himself maintains nothing of the sort. In his "Origin of Species" he says in the clearest terms that the struggle between the individuals of the same species does not at all happen in every species: "There must in every case be a struggle for existence, either one individual with another of the same species, or with the individuals of distinct species, or with the physical conditions of life."

The explanation of the second hypothesis, that of the evolution from egoism towards altruism, is more complicated. In the first place the facts adduced in support of it are not numerous, and they serve rather to illustrate a theory than to furnish the materials by which it may be justified. In the second place a part of the ethnological materials in relation to the question it has been impossible to utilize. They have been collected partly by persons convinced beforehand of the superiority of Christian morality to every other system, and who consequently disapprove of everything opposed to it, and partly by persons whose own conduct has caused the enmity manifested by the peoples with whom they have come into contact. No part of the history of civilization offers a more hideous spectacle than that of colonization. In the third place it is necessary to exclude peoples that have had much contact with Europeans or other civilized peoples. In the fourth place we often lose sight of the fact that primitive peoples show great differences of development, and consequently cannot be placed in the same rank. For example, if peoples despotically governed show strong egoistic tendencies, we have no right to declare that all primitive peoples are egoistic.

Finally it is the highest importance in studying primitive peoples to make the distinction between the acts which have to do with persons of the same social group, and those which have to do with strangers. One of the principal causes of the charge of egoism made against primitive peoples is to be found in the fact that this dualism of ethics is forgotten. In the passages I have cited . . . , the great difference between acts committed within and without the group is brought out. We have seen that the Indians of North America, although very altruistic toward those who form the same group with them, as also toward their guests, are the most pitiless enemies of those who attack their independence or their hunting ground. Now it has been by these last acts that these peoples have been generally judged, a wholly wrong method, since the "dualism of ethics" has always existed. Great would be the astonishment if any one were to maintain that the South African war proved that the English were a nation of murderers and incendiaries. Yet this is just the sort of reasoning that is applied to primitive peoples.

      ❖   ❖   ❖

One of the principal characteristics of social animals is the pleasure they experience in living in common, so that a social animal is unhappy if he is separate from those of the group in which he lives. Further it is necessary that the animal that cannot live alone, and is happy with his group, should also feel a sympathy with that group. Pleasure or its opposite felt by any individual reacts upon the whole group. A social being will try then to favor the interests of his fellows as far as he can, and in so far as he comprehends these interests. This sympathy will not extend to the whole species but only to the group. The general interest of the group does not permit the sympathy to embrace the whole species, but on the contrary requires one group to fight the other if, for example, the latter interferes with its food-supply. And even within the limits of the group the general interest may demand that a sick or wounded individual be abandoned, when by its presence it would for example, attract beasts of prey, and thus put the existence of all in danger.

Highly developed sympathy produces the spirit of sacrifice, which impels the individual to assist his companions sometimes even at the risk of his life. This quality is reinforced by the desire of gaining the praise and avoiding the blame of companions, which desire in its turn is brought about only by the life in common. For the one that lives in conjunction with others, and takes pleasure in doing so, whose interests are those of the members of the group, must be sensible of the approval or disapproval of his acts felt by others, since their feelings of pleasure or displeasure react upon himself. The lack of the power of speech among animals, however, limits the force of praise or blame among them.

We come now to the question: what are the causes of altruism among men? It must be considered as certain that man has always lived in groups more or less large, and it is even very probable that he is descended from animals equally social. A study of the means man has of sustaining the struggle for existence proves that they are of such a nature that he would have succumbed if he had lived in isolation. Kautsky puts it thus: ". . . man . . . whose mightiest and most effective, almost whose only weapon, indeed, in the struggle for existence, is association. He is, to be sure, distinguished above other animals by his intelligence, but this too is to the fruit of society, for in isolation he becomes dull and stupid. All man's other weapons in the struggle for existence are less efficient than those of the beasts. He has no weapons of attack like the beasts of prey, nor is he protected by his size like the elephant, hippopotamus and rhinoceros. He lacks the quickness of the squirrel and deer, and cannot repair his losses through superabundant fertility."

It is therefore on account of his constitution and of the struggle that he has had to sustain for his existence that man is a social being; in other words, those who showed social instincts stronger than the others ran less danger of succumbing in the contest for life, and had more chance of transmitting their leanings to their posterity. As man has greater intellectual capacities than the animals he is more capable of understanding the joys and sorrows of his fellows, and so is better able to assist the one and avoid the other. In the second place he has a developed language at his command, through which a great influence can be exercised upon conduct by blame and praise.

The fact that man is born with social instincts does not, however, explain altruism sufficiently, for among animal species there is not one whose individuals have done so much harm to one another as men, who, though they are social beings, are capable of committing the most egoistic acts. How shall we explain these contradictions?

We have seen above that primitive peoples to whom we have referred showed very altruistic traits of character. The members of a group extend mutual aid, and, in their relations with one another, are benevolent, honest, truthful, and very susceptible to the opinions of others, etc.

It is impossible to explain this either by the race to which these peoples belong or by the climate in which they live, for they are of different races (for example North American Indians and the Hindoos of the delta of the Ganges) and live under different climates (as the Eskimos and the South American Indians). Besides this some of these peoples show towards strangers qualities directly contrary to those they display toward members of their own group. Thus, as we have already remarked, the North American Indians are most cruel enemies, most pitiless toward those who are not of their group, while they are quite the reverse toward their own fellow-tribesmen. It is plain, then, that their altruistic sentiments have nothing to do with race or climate.

Consequently the cause can only be found in the social environment, which is determined in its turn by the mode of production. What follows will show that in the last instance it is the mode of production that is able to develop the social predisposition innate in man (not in the same measure for each individual, which is a question that I shall return to) or prevent this disposition from being developed, or may even destroy it entirely. Upon examining the modes of production in force among the peoples cited we see that they are characterized by the following traits, very different from those of the present system.

The first of these characteristic traits is this: *production takes place among these peoples for personal consumption and not for exchange as with us.* It has often been claimed that the primitive peoples lived in a state of communism. Taken in the sense of a communism in production this assertion is true only in part; except for hunts undertaken in common, production was not carried on in common but was individual. The weapons and utensils of the hunt were private property, while the hunting ground was held in common. Just so as soon as architectural technique made some progress the houses often became common property. At its inception agriculture was not practiced in common. It was only when it had attained a certain development that this was sometimes the case. But if we take communism in the sense of consumption in common, then the assertion becomes much more exact. I do not mean to say that consumption always took place in common (though several primitive peoples took their food in common), but when from whatever cause some members of the group had failed to produce, the other members who had been more fortunate provided for them. The productivity of labor was still small; there was not generally any surplus of labor. Even if there had been there could not have been any possibility of exchange, since the division of labor was very slight, and consequently each one was capable of making for himself what others would have been able to offer in exchange.

The second characteristic of the modes of production of the peoples in question is bound up with the first, namely that *there was neither wealth nor poverty.* If there was privation (through scarcity of game, for example), all suffered; if there was abundance, all profited by it.

The third fact to be noted is that *the subordination of man to nature was very great,* so great that we, who have so largely subjugated the forces of nature, can have no idea of it. If primitive men were very weak in their contest with nature even when joined together in a single group, individually they were absolutely unable to maintain the struggle, and were thus forced to unite.

If we consider the characteristics of the primitive modes of production, it becomes clear, it seems to me, why the primitive peoples were not more egoistic. They had neither rich nor poor; their economic interests were either parallel or equal (the latter in the case of production in common); the economic life, therefore, did not arouse egoistic ideas—they were not led into temptation. Where the economic system does not produce egoistic ideas it accustoms men to being unegoistic, and if their interests do happen occasionally to conflict, the matter is looked at altruistically and not egoistically. And since the economic life is the "conditio sine qua non" of life in general, and thus occupies the important place in human existence, it stamps the whole life with its non-egoistic character. Since the struggle for existence must be sustained in common against nature, if it is to be efficacious it binds human interests so closely together that they are inseparable; the interest of one is the same as that of his comrade.

We shall now understand why primitive men feel themselves to be first of all the members of a unit; why they not only abstain from acts harmful to their companions, but come to their aid whenever they can; why they are honest, benevolent, and truthful towards the members of their group, and why public opinion has so great an influence among them—characteristics which the quotations that I have already made have established. The cause of these facts is to be found in *the mode of production, which brought about a uniformity of interest in the persons united in a single group, obliged them to aid one another in the difficult and uninterrupted struggle for existence, and made men free and equal, since there was neither poverty nor riches, and consequently no possibility of oppression.*

It is only in such an environment that the social instincts innate in man can be developed, and the more the mode of production

binds men's interests together the greater will this development
be. It is a truth as old as the world that one respects the interests
of others and does not deceive them, only when these others do
not make life more difficult, but aid in supporting it. If not, social
instincts will be suppressed and the contrary instincts formed.
The development of the social feelings is based upon reciprocity.
When this is lacking these feelings lie dormant, but when reciprocity exists they grow stronger by constantly reacting from one
to the other.

There is still another reason which helped strengthen the
solidarity among the members of the same group. The primitive
peoples, who practiced agriculture little or not at all, needed an
immense territory to provide for their needs. Lands whose population would seem small to the Europeans of our day, had in
reality as dense a population as the mode of production would
permit. From this there sprang continual wars between groups
disputing the possession of a certain territory. The necessity of
defending as a body the territory acquired, or of conquering it
anew, resulted in drawing always tighter the bonds uniting the
members of the same group.

The same mode of production which drew the members of a
group into an altruistic solidarity, forced these same persons into
a position of excessive egoism toward those who did not belong
to their group and opposed them in obtaining what they needed.
The same act, killing an enemy for example, is the most egoistic
act possible from the point of view of the enemy but a very
altruistic act from the point of view of the slayer, since he has
increased the security of his group. The development of the
social feelings is, then, only determined by the form of the
struggle for existence.

How then shall we explain certain egoistic acts directed
against members of the same group? How, for example, can the
infanticide so common among primitive peoples be explained?
In seeking for a solution we shall see that this egoistic act does

not result from innate insensibility toward children (the contrary is true, as we have seen above), but from the fact that the limited control over nature makes a great increase in the population impossible. The children were killed immediately after birth; no one dreamed of ridding himself of a child of greater age. Further, the nomadic life prevented the carrying along of a great number of children.

It is for the same reason that the sick and the aged were sometimes abandoned by the primitive peoples. They were driven to this because these feeble persons were unable to make long journeys, and because their economic means did not allow them to support those who could no longer work. Here again there could be no question of innate insensibility. In these cases then, there was an opposition of interests; the act that was egoistic toward the individual was altruistic toward the group. If different action had been taken in such cases all would have succumbed. Thus these acts have fallen into desuetude as the productivity of labor has developed.

The continual development of the productivity of labor has modified the structure of society greatly. As soon as productivity has increased to such an extent that the producer can regularly produce more than he needs, and the division of labor puts him in a position to exchange the surplus for things that he could not produce himself, at this moment there arises in man the notion of no longer giving to his comrades what they need, but of keeping for himself the surplus of what his labor produces, and exchanging it. Then it is that the mode of production begins to run counter to the social instincts of man instead of favoring it as heretofore.

✿   ✿   ✿

However, this is only one side of the question. Through the development of exchange not only does man become egoistic toward those who for any reason are unable to provide for their needs, but exchange itself is an entirely egoistic act for the two parties who enter into it. Each tries to get as much profit for himself as possible, and consequently to make the other lose. The existence of economic laws which in many, and even in most cases prevent the two parties from injuring each other, does not change the fact at all. Commerce weakens the social instincts of man; the loss of one becomes the gain of another. When two persons are trading there springs up a tendency on the part of each to overvalue his own property and to disparage that of the other; commerce is one of the important causes of lying. In addition to this tendency another arises, that of giving goods of quality inferior to that agreed upon; the constant attention to one's own interests produces and develops fraud.

The more production for one's own use decreases, and the greater becomes the production for exchange, the more do habit and tradition produce in men the characteristics mentioned. As soon as exchange has developed to a certain point commerce begins to be a special trade. The merchant is much more exposed to the conditions named than those who trade only occasionally. Not only does he pass a great part of his life in exchanging but he is by profession egoistic in two directions; toward the producer from whom he buys, and toward the consumer to whom he sells.

When it reaches a certain height the continually increasing productivity of labor brings a further important modification in the social structure, namely slavery. For this springs up when production is so advanced that man can regularly produce more than he actually needs for himself, and when it is possible for him to exchange the overplus for things which he can use but cannot make. Prisoners of war are no longer killed as formerly, but are obliged to work for the profit of the conquerors. In this way is formed a considerable opposition of interest between two classes of individuals who together form a social unit: on the one hand those who, deprived of one of the most important factors of human happiness, liberty, are obliged to exhaust themselves for the benefit of others, and have only the strict necessaries of life; and on the other hand those who profit by the enslavement and excessive labor of the first.

Slavery (with the other forms of forced service, serfdom and wage-labor) is one of the most important factors that undermine the social instincts in man. Slavery, runs the saying, demoralizes the master as well as the slave. It arouses in the master the notion that the slave is not a thinking and feeling man like himself, but an instrument destined exclusively to be useful to him. In the slave himself it kills the feeling of independence; lacking the arms which the free man has at his disposal, the slave has recourse to dissimulation to defend himself against his master.

The overplus which one person can obtain by his own labor must always remain limited. Without the rise of slavery the great wealth of a single individual would not have been possible. To the difference between master and slave is now added that between rich and poor, and the envy and hatred of the poor for the rich, and the pride of the rich and their desire to dominate over the poor. Since the division of society into rich and poor the aristocracy has been formed, which does not owe its origin to the excellence of its members, as one might imagine from this inaccurate name, but to their wealth.

The period of civilization during which the social modification mentioned above has taken place is generally lauded to the skies, as compared with preceding epochs. In certain relations this is justifiable. Technique has made immense progress and especially during the last phase of civilization, capitalism; the power of man over nature has advanced greatly; the productivity of labor has been so increased that one class of men, exempted by this from permanent care for their daily bread, are able to devote themselves to the arts and sciences. All this is indisputable. But the development of the arts and sciences and of technique has only an indirect importance for the etiology of crime. The question first of all to be asked is this: What influence has this modification in the economic and social structure had upon the character of man? And the answer to this question can only be the following: this modification has engendered cupidity and ambition, has made man less sensitive to the happiness and misery of his fellows, and has decreased the influence exercised upon men's acts by the opinions of others. In short, it has developed egoism at the expense of altruism.

C. Egoistic Tendencies Resulting from the Present Economic System and from Its Consequences

The etiology of crime includes the three following problems;

First. Whence does the criminal thought in man arise?

Second. What forces are there in man which can prevent the execution of this criminal thought, and what is their origin?

Third. What is the occasion for the commission of criminal acts. (As the occasion may be one of the causes of the criminal thought, problems one and three at times form but one.)

- For the moment we are still occupied with general considerations with regard to crime; it is clear then that the first and third questions will be examined only when we are treating of crimes according to the groups into which they must be divided because of the great differences which their nature presents.

It is otherwise with the second question. As we have seen in the preceding pages, it is certain that man is born with social instincts, which, when influenced by a favorable environment can exert a force great enough to prevent egoistic thoughts from leading to egoistic acts. And since crime constitutes a part of the egoistic acts, it is of importance, for the etiology of *crime in general*, to inquire whether the present method of production and its social consequences are an obstacle to the development of the social instincts, and in what measure. We shall try in the following pages to show the influence of the economic system and of these consequences upon the social instincts of man.

After what we have just said it is almost superfluous to remark that the egoistic tendency does not *by itself* make a man criminal. For this something else is necessary. It is possible for the environment to create a great egoist, but this does not imply that the egoist will necessarily become criminal. For example, a man who is enriched by the exploitation of children may nevertheless remain all his life an honest man from the legal point of view. He does not think of stealing, because he has a surer and more lucrative means of getting wealth, although he lacks the moral sense which would prevent him from committing a crime if the thought of it occurred to him. We shall show that, as a consequence of the present environment, man has become very egoistic and hence more *capable of crime,* than if the environment had developed the germs of altruism.

a. The present economic system is based upon exchange. As we saw at the end of the preceding section such a mode of production cannot fail to have an egoistic character. A society based upon exchange isolates the individuals by weakening the bond that unites them. When it is a question of exchange the two parties interested think only of their own advantage, even to the detriment of the other party. In the second place the possibility of exchange arouses in a man the thought of the possibility of converting the surplus of his labor into things which increase his well-being in place of giving the benefit of it to those who are deprived of the necessaries of life. Hence the possibility of exchange gives birth to cupidity.

The exchange called simple circulation of commodities is practiced by all men as consumers, and by the workers besides as vendors of their labor power. However, the influence of this simple circulation of commodities is weak compared with that exercised by capitalistic exchange. It is only the exchange of the surplus of labor, by the producer, for other commodities, and hence is for him a secondary matter. As a result he does not exchange with a view to profit (though he tries to make as advantageous a trade as possible), but to get things which he cannot produce himself.

Capitalistic exchange, on the other hand, has another aim— that of making a profit. A merchant, for example, does not buy goods for his own use, but to sell them to advantage. He will, then, always try, on the one hand, to buy the best commodities as cheaply as possible, by depreciating them as much as he can; on the other hand, to make the purchaser pay as high a price as possible, by exaggerating the value of his wares. *By the nature of the mode of production itself* the merchant is therefore forced to make war upon two sides, must maintain his own interests against the interests of those with whom he does business. If he does not injure too greatly the interests of those from whom he buys, and those to whom he sells, it is for the simple reason that these would otherwise do business with those of his competitors who do not find their interest in fleecing their customers. Wherever competition is eliminated for whatever cause the tactics of the merchant are shown in their true light; he thinks only of his own advantage even to the detriment of those with whom he does business. "No commerce without trickery" is a proverbial expression (among consumers), and with the ancients Mercury, the god of commerce, was also the god of thieves. This is true, that the merchant and the thief are alike in taking account *exclusively* of their own interest to the detriment of those with whom they have to do.

The fact that in our present society production does not take place generally to provide for the needs of men, but for many other reasons, has important effects upon the character of those who possess the means of production. Production is carried on for profit exclusively; if greater profits can be made by stopping production it will be stopped—this is the point of view of the capitalists. The consumers, on the other hand, see in the production the means of creating what man has need of. The world likes to be deceived, and does not care to recognize the fact that the producer has only his own profit in view. The latter encourages this notion and poses as a disinterested person. If he reduces the price of his wares, he claims to do it in the interest of the public, and takes care not to admit that it is for the purpose of increasing his own profits. This is the falsity that belongs inevitably to capitalism.

In general this characteristic of capitalism has no importance for the morality of the consumer, who is merely duped, but it is far otherwise with the press, which is almost entirely in the power of the capitalists. The press, which ought to be a guide for the masses, and is so in some few cases, in the main is in the hands of capitalists who use it only as a means of making money. In place of being edited by men who, by their ability and firmness, are capable of enlightening the public, newspapers are carried on by persons who see in their calling only a livelihood, and consider only the proprietor of the sheet. In great part the press is the opposite of what it ought to be; it represents the interests of those who pay for advertisements or for articles; it increases the ignorance and the prejudices of the crowd; in a word, it poisons public opinion.

Besides this general influence upon the public the press has further a special place in the etiology of crime, from the fact that most newspapers, in order to satisfy the morbid curiosity of the public, relate all great crimes in extenso, give portraits of the victims, etc., and are often one of the causes of new crimes, by arousing the imitative instinct to be found in man.

As we have seen above the merchant capitalist makes war in two directions; his interests are against those of the man who sells to him, and of the man who buys from him. This is also true of the industrialist capitalist. He buys raw materials and sells what he produces. But to arrive at his produce he must buy labor, and this purchase is "sui generis."

Deprived as he is of the means of production the working-man sells his labor only in order not to die of hunger. The capitalist takes advantage of this necessitous condition of the worker and exploits him. We have already indicated that capitalism has this trait in common with the earlier methods of production. Little by little one class of men has become accustomed to think that the others are destined to amass wealth for them and to be subservient to them in every way. Slavery, like the wage system, demoralizes the servant as well as the master. With the master it develops cupidity and the imperious character which sees in a fellow man only a being fit to satisfy his desires. It is true that the capitalist has not the power over the proletarian that the master has over his slave; he has neither the right of service nor the power of life and death, yet it is none the less true that he has another weapon against the proletarian, a weapon whose effect is no less terrible, namely enforced idleness. The fact that the supply of manual labor always greatly exceeds the demand puts this weapon into the hands of every capitalist. It is not only the capitalists who carry on any business that are subjected to this influence, but also all who are salaried in their service.

Capitalism exercises in still a third manner an egoistic influence upon the capitalistic "entrepreneur." Each branch has more producers than are necessary. The interests of the capitalists are, then, opposed not only to those of the men from whom they buy or to whom they sell, but also to those of their fellow producers. It is indeed claimed that competition has the effect simply of making the product better and cheaper, but this is looking at the question from only one point of view. The fact which alone affects criminality is that competition forces the participants, under penalty of succumbing, to be as egoistic as possible. Even the producers who have the means of applying all the technical improvements to perfect their product and make it cheaper, are obliged to have recourse to gross deceits in advertising, etc., in order to injure their competitors. Rejoicing at the evil which befalls another, envy at his good fortune, these forms of egoism are the inevitable consequence of competition.

[We] . . . come now to that part of the bourgeoisie which, without having any occupation, consumes what has been made by others. Not to feel obliged to contribute to the material well-being of humanity in proportion to one's ability must necessarily have a demoralizing influence. A parasite, one who lives without working, does not feel bound by any moral tie to his fellows, but regards them simply as things, instruments meant to serve and amuse him. Their example is a source of demoralization for those about them, and excites the envy of those who see this easy life without the power of enjoying it themselves, and awakes in them the desire to exchange their painful existence for this "dolce far niente."

The egoistic tendencies work less strongly in the third group of the bourgeoisie, those who practice the liberal professions. However, the products of the arts and sciences having become commodities, the egoistic influence of exchange here too is not to be neglected. Then competition arising from overproduction is a great cause of demoralization, for where there is competition men become egoistic. So in the domain of the liberal professions competition often forces those who do not find a field of activity in accordance with their ideas, to work that is contrary to those ideas. Thus it is quite right to speak of a prostitution of the intellect.

Before concluding these observations upon the bourgeoisie there is still something to be said about politics. As we have seen above the state owes its origin to the formation of opposition of interests in society; the first task of the state being, therefore, the maintenance of a certain amount of order. This requires above all the holding of the great mass in subjection. As long as this mass is weak the dominant class has no need to resort to trickery; but as soon as the oppressed class can oppose the domination of the others, as soon as brutal power no longer gives the desired result, the dominant class changes its tactics. It attempts to create the impression that the concessions it has been forced to make are acts of charity; and presuming upon the ignorance of the oppressed, it pretends that their condition is not so bad, etc. Many of those engaged in politics play this part without being conscious of their duplicity. However, the contest between the classes exercises its baleful influence upon them also, for they involuntarily distort the facts, whereas the evolution of society has reached such a point that a new social order is necessary.

The power in the State sometimes passes from one party of the ruling class to another. All profit by the temporary opportunity not only for the realization of their political program, but also to procure advantages for their partisans. This struggle for power is carried on partly by means prejudicial to the character of those interested, while the end aimed at by some parties can be frankly avowed. It is for the same reason that international politics is such a source of lying and hypocrisy, the states not being able to avow their real intention—the weakening of their neighbors.

The proletariat. To be thorough we begin by making mention of one of the consequences of the economic position of the proletariat, of which we have already treated briefly, namely the dependence in which persons of this class find themselves in consequence of their lacking the means of production, a state which has a prejudicial influence upon character. The oppressed resort to means which they would otherwise scorn. As we have seen above, the basis of the social feelings is reciprocity. As soon as this is trodden under foot by the ruling class the social sentiments of the oppressed become weak towards them.

We come now . . . first to the consequences of the labor of the young. The paid labor of the young has a bad influence in several ways. First, it forces them, while they are still very young, to think only of their own interests; then, brought into contact with persons who are rough and indifferent to their well-being, they follow these only too quickly, because of their imitative tendencies, in their bad habits, grossness of speech, etc. Finally, the paid labor of the young makes them more or less independent at an age where they have the greatest need of guidance. Even if the statistical proof of the influence of the labor of children and young people upon criminality were totally wanting, no one could deny that influence. Child labor is entirely a capitalistic phenomenon, being found especially in the great manufacturing countries like England and Germany. And then one of the most salient facts of criminality is the amount of juvenile crime, which is so enormous that England, followed by other countries, has established a special system to combat this form of criminality. Certainly this increase of juvenile crime is chiefly due to the influence of bad domestic conditions (wage-labor of married women, etc.), but the labor of the young people themselves also plays its part.

*   *   *

Keeping constantly in mind that in our days juvenile criminals are less often sentenced than formerly, we shall find that the foregoing statistics show:

First. That juvenile crime is increasing.

Second. That this increase is considerable in the countries like Germany, Austria, and Belgium, where there is a continuous industrial development; while in countries less developed industrially the increase is less.

Third. That England, where the capitalism is very intense, shows a great amount of juvenile crime.

The figures we have given have in general, in my opinion, gone to support the incontestable truth, that there is a relation between child labor and juvenile criminality. Although it is of smaller importance than the lack of care of the children among the proletariat, it is still one of the factors in the etiology of crime.

[We] . . . come now to the influence of long hours of labor. It has rightly been said that work has a strong moral influence. But it is also true that immoderate labor has the contrary effect. It brutalizes a man, makes him incapable of elevated sentiments, kills . . . the man in the beast, while moderate labor ennobles the beast in the man.

The housing conditions of the proletariat have also a significance as regards criminality, and for the special group of sexual offenses their importance is very great. We shall speak of this more fully when we treat especially of these offenses, and will, for the moment, note simply their general consequences.

The disorder and squalor of the home communicate themselves to the inmates; the lack of room obliges the children to live, during a great part of the day, on the streets, with the result that they are brought into contact with all sorts of demoralizing companions. Finally, the living together of a great number of uneducated persons in one small dwelling is the cause of constant quarrels and fights. The situation of those who are merely night-lodgers is especially unfortunate, as we have already seen.

❉   ❉   ❉

As has already been said at the beginning of these observations as to the influence of the economic life upon the development of social feelings on the part of the proletariat, the egoistic side of the human character is developed by the fact that the individual is dependent, that he lives in a subordinate position, and that he feels himself poor and deprived of everything. However, in so far as the proletarian sells his labor he is guaranteed against famine, however miserable his condition, and conscious of the utility of his rôle in society, he feels himself, notwithstanding his poverty, a man who, except for his employer, is independent of all men. But if work is not to be found, or if the proletarian, sick and infirm, is not able to work, it goes without saying that the resulting unemployment is very demoralizing. The lack of steady work, the horrors of the penury into which he and his fall, and the long train of evils which result from both, kill the social feelings in a man, for, as we have seen above, these feelings depend upon reciprocity. Let one familiarize himself with the thought of the condition of the man who lives in the greatest poverty, *i.e.*, the man who is abandoned by all, and he will understand how egoistic must be the feelings of such.

From the position in which the proletarians find themselves it follows that, towards each other, it is rather the altruistic than the egoistic feelings that develop; living less isolated than the bourgeois, they see the misfortune that strikes their neighbor, and have felt the same themselves, and above all, their economic interests are not opposed. Forced idleness—at present chronic, and acute in times of panic—modifies these conditions at times; it makes competitors of the workers, who take the bread out of each other's mouths.

The proletarian is never sure of his existence: like the sword of Damocles unemployment is constantly hanging over his head. Upon this subject Engels says:

"But far more demoralizing than his poverty in its influence upon the English working man is the insecurity of his position, the necessity of living upon wages from hand to mouth, that in short which makes a proletarian of him. The smaller peasants in Germany are usually poor, and often suffer want, but they are less at the mercy of accident, they have at least something secure. The proletarian, who has nothing but his two hands, who consumes today what he earned yesterday, who is subject to every chance, and has not the slightest guarantee for being able to earn the barest necessities of life, whom every crisis, every whim of his employer may deprive of bread, this proletarian is placed in the most revolting, inhuman position conceivable for a human being."

This uncertainty of existence is one of the reasons which explain why, in relatively prosperous times the working-man often spends his wages as soon as he receives them, for he knows that the economies possible to him are so small that he could never be saved from misery in case of unemployment.

Finally we must speak of ignorance and lack of training on the part of the proletariat, as a factor of criminality. As we know, this question of education is one of those which are most debated in criminal sociology. Certain authors have prophesied that each new school would make a prison superfluous, while on the other hand it has been claimed that ignorance and the lack of civilization have nothing to do with the etiology of crime, but that on the contrary knowledge and civilization are even factors of crime. Although these extreme opinions are hardly ever expressed nowadays, the ideas upon the point in question still differ widely.

In my opinion, no really decisive arguments have ever been adduced for the opinion that the intellectual condition of men has no influence upon criminality. In general the reasoning is as follows: ignorance is decreasing; crime on the contrary increases; ignorance cannot therefore be a factor. Such a line of argument is very superficial, for ignorance is surely not the only cause of crime. Its influence may therefore be neutralized by other factors. And further, from the point of view of statistics it is not permissible to use the indirect method when the direct method is practicable. In most criminal and prison statistics the percentage of the illiterate among the criminals is given, and we have only to put beside these figures those for the illiterate among the non-criminal population to be convinced of the existence or absence of the connection in dispute.

*   *   *

I am of the opinion that the statistics which I have quoted, including, as they do, millions of criminals, are very significant:

the illiterates supply, in general, a great proportion of the criminals, a proportion much greater than that of the illiterates in the general population.

❄   ❄   ❄

The ancient idea that crime is only a consequence of ignorance need not be treated of, for morality and intellect are two distinct parts of the psychic life, even though there exists a certain relation between them.

The first reason why ignorance and the lack of general culture must be ranked among the general factors of crime is this: the person who, in our present society, where the great majority of parents care very little for the education of their children, does not go to school, is deprived of the moral ideas (honesty, etc.) which are taught there, and ordinarily passes his time in idleness and vagabondage.

The second reason which makes ignorance a factor of crime, is that generally an ignorant man is, more than others, a man moved by the impulse of the moment, who allows himself to be governed by his passions, and is induced to commit acts which he would not have committed if his intellectual equipment had been different.

In the third place, it is for the following reasons that ignorance and the lack of training fall within the etiology of crime. The mind of the man whose psychic qualities, whether in the domain of the arts, or of the sciences, have been developed, has become less susceptible to evil ideas. His intellectual condition constitutes thus a bridle which can restrain evil thoughts from realizing themselves; for real art and true science strengthen the social instincts. The figures cited above furnish only a slight contribution to this question. There is no doubt that if we had figures showing how many criminals there are any part of whose life is taken up by art or science, we should find the number very small. It could not be objected that the cause of this is in the innate qualities of the criminals; certainly one man is born with greater capacity than another, but everyone is born with some capacities which, if developed, may become a source of happiness; and a happy man, says the proverb, is not wicked.

Finally ignorance is in still another way a factor in crime. Very often the author of a crime conceives and executes it in so clumsy a fashion and with so little chance of success, that we may be certain that he would not have committed it if he had not been an ignorant person, without knowledge of the forces with which he had to do.

When the Italian school is reproached with making their researches upon prisoners only, and not upon criminals and their free equals, the implication is that it is only the stupid and ignorant criminals that are in prison, while the others, the shrewd and tricky, remain at liberty. There is assuredly much truth in this assertion.

The lower proletariat. In the preceding pages I have already spoken of the influence exercised by bad material surroundings upon a man's character; I have pointed out the moral consequences of bad housing conditions, and also that he becomes embittered and malicious through lack of the necessaries of life. All this applies to the proletariat in general, but much more strongly still to those who do not succeed, for any reason, in selling their labor, that is the lower proletariat.

If the dwellings of the working-class are bad, those of the lower proletariat are more pitiable still. There are, through sickness or lack of work, periods of dire poverty in the life of almost every worker—for the lower proletariat these periods are without intermission. Its poverty is chronic. And when the poverty makes itself felt for a long time together, the intellectual faculties become blunted to such a point that there remains of the man only the brute, struggling for existence.

Although the material and intellectual poverty of the lower proletariat is much greater than that of the proletariat, the difference between them is only quantitative. In one connection, however, there is also a qualitative difference, and a very important one, namely that the working-man is a useful being without whom society could not exist. However oppressed he may be, he is a man who has a feeling of self-respect. It is different with the member of the lower proletariat. He is not useful, but a detriment. He produces nothing, and tries to live upon what others make; he is merely tolerated. He who has lived long in poverty loses all feeling of self-respect, and lends himself to anything whatever that will suffice to prolong his existence.

In short, poverty (taken in the sense of absolute want), kills the social sentiments in man, destroys in fact all relations between men. He who is abandoned by all can no longer have any feeling for those who have left him to his fate.

h. The proportion in which the different classes are guilty of crime. After having treated of the direct consequences of the present economic system upon the different classes, I shall take up this question, which is an important one for the problem of criminality, before touching upon the indirect consequences.

❋   ❋   ❋

All the statistics cited show then that the poor supply a very great proportion of the convicts, in every case a greater proportion than they bear to the population in general, and the well-to-do form only a small part.

There are still other ways of inquiring what part the different classes take in criminality. One consists in an examination of the statistics of the intellectual development of the convicts, for the illiterate and those who have received only a primary education belong, almost without exception, to the classes without fortune. These statistics have already been given, and they confirm entirely the conclusions to be drawn from the figures for the financial condition of the convicts.

The third way of solving the problem is by a study of the

statistics of the occupations of those convicted. Here, however, great difficulties present themselves. In the first place not all the criminal statistics make the distinction between the employer and the workman in such and such an occupation. And it is just this information that we need. In the second place we need beside statistics for the occupation of the criminals, others showing the occupations of the population in general, and the two classified in the same way. Even in this case the picture given by these statistics will not be exact, for there are among the employers many persons who are not really independent (workers at home, etc.), or persons who, while being employers, are, as far as their plane of living is concerned, only the equal of the proletarian, and not of the bourgeois.

❊   ❊   ❊

We have now arrived at the end of our observations upon occupations among criminals. Other statistics are available, but either it is impossible to compare them with statistics of the non-criminal population, or they are without significance for some other reason. At any rate it seems to me that those I have given are enough to show that proportionately the non-possessors are more guilty of crime than the possessors.

The thesis set forth above is confirmed, then, in three different ways. The question still remains to be answered, to what must we attribute the greater criminality among the non-possessors?

As was remarked at the beginning of this section (on the egoistic tendency of the present economic system, and its consequences), there are three questions which present themselves in connection with the etiology of crime; first, what is the origin of the criminal idea? Second, what are the forces in man which prevent this idea from coming to realization? Third, the occasion for committing the crime. For the moment we shall concern ourselves with the second question only; and we shall ask ourselves the question, is the explanation that these forces are weaker with non-possessors than with others? It is very difficult, if not impossible, to give an answer to this question, for it is very complicated. In the first place it is necessary to prove that the environment of the non-possessors arouses thoughts for which that of the possessors offers no place. The circumstances in which the well-to-do live are in general of such a nature that the moral force has no need of offering combat, since the criminal thought does not exist. For example, in economic offenses one of the principal provocatives of criminal ideas is poverty, which is unknown to the bourgeoisie. It follows that nothing definite can be said about the relative force of the moral sentiments in these two groups of the population in counteracting criminal ideas. Other examples could be added, and I am of the opinion that this influence of the environment will be by itself sufficient to explain the difference in the criminality of the two groups.

It is impossible to decide with certainty whether, aside from the above-mentioned influence of the environment, the present economic system and its consequences have a harmful influence upon the social sentiments that is stronger in the case of non-possessors than it is in the case of possessors. It must be considered as certain . . . that the circumstances in which children and young people live among the proletariat is a cause of their being much more demoralized than the children of the bourgeoisie. The influences acting upon the adults of the two classes differ so much in nature and intensity that it is impossible to contrast their effects.

It is unnecessary to say that in what has preceded the possessing class has been contrasted with the proletariat alone, and not with the lower proletariat. It goes without saying that the environment in which the latter live makes them the class most destitute of the moral sense in the whole population.

c. Marriage. To form an idea as to whether there is a relation between crime and marriage, and in this case, as to what its nature is, we must have recourse to statistics.

*   *   *

After an examination of the results found it is impossible to say that the married persons show absolutely a criminality less in degree than that of the unmarried; there is a variation for offenses as well as for ages. Only considered in general, the tendency to crime is less in the case of the married than of the unmarried.

As the following figures prove, the connection between crime and marriage is quite different in the case of women.

*   *   *

The conclusion to be drawn is that the married woman commits more crimes than the unmarried, but that this does not apply to all crimes nor to all ages.

So much for the figures themselves; now for their explanation.

It is very difficult, in examining the influence of marriage upon criminality, to separate the moral consequences from other factors. We are mistaken, for example, if we attribute to the moral influence of marriage the fact that married persons are less often guilty of the great majority of economic crimes than the unmarried. The fact that anyone marries is ordinarily an indication that he is in a material situation more or less good. The danger that he will commit an economic offense becomes, then, much less great than when he is in a less comfortable condition. The correctness of this position is clearly shown by the statistics given, according to which married men still young give a higher figure than that furnished by the bachelors. The reason is that proletarians marry while still young. The material cares of these husbands are then much greater than later on when their children have already left home, or are at least earning their own living. If we examine the figures for insults we shall see that married men and women both are more guilty than the unmarried. It would be very erroneous to conclude that marriage increases the tendency to this offense. The explanation is to be found in the fact that when a single dwelling (or barrack rather) is the common habitation of several workmen's families, living conditions easily become a permanent source of disputes. In this case it is not marriage but bad housing conditions which appear as a factor in the etiology of crime. If it were possible to separate these conditions or these material consequences of marriage from its moral consequences, the difference between the criminality of the married and the unmarried would not appear very great. Especially is this true if we keep sight of the fact that the bourgeoisie generally marry at a more advanced age than the proletariat. This brings it about that there are more of the bourgeois among the older married people than among the younger; and since, from other causes, the bourgeoisie commit fewer crimes than the proletariat, the influence of marriage seems greater here than it really is.

As for the criminality of women it must be noted that the unmarried women of the bourgeoisie represent a greater proportion of the whole number of unmarried women than the women of this class do of women in general. And since from other causes the criminality of the women of this last class is very small, marriage seems to have a less favorable effect than it really has.

As for the consequences of marriage upon morality, I believe they are the following. In the first place marriage has a tendency to increase the feeling of responsibility, especially if there are children. Then when man and wife understand one another, when they are happy in their union, no one will deny that marriage has a strong moral influence, for, according to the proverb, happy people are not wicked. The proof of this is that married men participate less than bachelors in the crimes of rebellion, assault, homicide, murder, etc., while widowers are more often guilty of them, becoming addicted to alcohol after the death of their wives, or becoming demoralized in other ways. However, it would be more accurate to speak of the moral influence of love than of marriage in the sense of legal monogamy. Happy married couples do not owe their happiness to the legal sanction. Without it their happiness would be as great. On the other hand if the couple is ill-assorted for one reason or another, then marriage has a very demoralizing influence. Legal monogamy comes into play in such cases by rendering difficult the separation of persons who do not understand each other, or of whom one or the other conducts himself badly.

The great power of a man over his wife, as a consequence of his economic preponderance, may equally be a demoralizing cause. It is certain that there will always be abuse of power on the part of a number of those whom social circumstances have clothed with a certain authority. How many women there are now who have to endure the coarseness and bad treatment of their husbands, but would not hesitate to leave them if their economic dependence and the law did not prevent. Holmes, the author of "Pictures and Problems from London Police Courts", who for years saw all the unfortunates who came before these tribunals, says in this connection: "A good number of Englishmen seem to think they have as perfect a right to thrash or kick their wives as the American had to 'lick his nigger.' Yes, and some of these fellows are completely astonished when a magistrate ventures to hold a different opinion. I well remember a great hulking fellow, with a leg-of-mutton fist, being charged with assaulting a policeman. After all the evidence had been given, the magistrate inquired whether the prisoner had been previously charged. 'Yes, your worship, he was here two months ago, charged with assaulting a female.' As the prisoner declared this was false, and indignantly denied that he had ever assaulted a female, the gaoler brought in his book and proved the conviction. The prisoner then looked up in astonishment, and said:

'Oh, why, it was only my own wife!' Only their own wives; but how those wives suffer! Is there any misery equal to theirs, any slavery to compare with theirs? If so, I never heard of it. I have seen thousands of them, and their existence is our shame and degradation."

Further it goes without saying that a marriage entered into for reasons of self-interest is demoralizing.

Although the above consequences of marriage must be mentioned, that our discussion may be as complete as possible, and although they may have a certain importance for the etiology of crime, yet their influence is not very great. There are causes of criminality much more important, which may put those that have been named entirely in the shade.

Before taking up the criminal consequences of the family, I am of the opinion that this is the best place to fix our attention for a moment upon the criminality of women. In treating above of the origin of marriage as it exists today, we have at the same time spoken of the social position of woman.

d. The criminality of women. In order to give an idea of its extent and nature we must begin with some statistics.

*   *   *

Here, then, are the facts, which may be reduced to this, that in all the countries named the criminality of women is much less than that of men. However, it is greater than we should suppose from the figures, since almost all the figures (except those for France) have to do with persons convicted, and acquittal is much more common in the case of women than in that of men.

*   *   *

Other reasons why the criminality of women seems smaller than it really is are the following: As is shown by the statistics cited, the offenses of which women are most often guilty, are also those which it is most difficult to discover, namely those committed without violence. Then, those who have been injured are less likely to bring a complaint against a woman than against a man. But even when we take account of all these things, the criminality of women remains much smaller than that of men. This may be explained as follows:

First. An examination of the tables shows that women participate less in the crimes which require strength or courage. The first cause is to be found in the fact, then, that the average woman of our time has less strength and courage than the average man, and consequently commits on the average fewer crimes than he.

Second. It is clear that women take small part in sexual crimes (for procuration is not a sexual crime but an economic one), which is to be explained by the fact that most sexual crimes cannot, from their nature, be committed by women. Another reason is that the rôle of women in the sexual life (and thus in the criminal sexual life) is rather passive than active.

Third. The small part played by women in economic crimes committed because of poverty or even of greed, is explained by prostitution, which generally yields greater and more certain returns than crime, and avoids the risk of prison.

Fourth. A comparison of the criminal statistics of different countries has not much value for the different reasons already given. . . . Only when the figures are very different may one draw a conclusion from them. A comparison of the tables brings out the fact that the criminality of women does not differ much in the countries named. However, when we fix our attention upon the crimes and misdemeanors more or less grave in the Italian statistics (assizes and correctional tribunals) we discover that there is a considerable difference between England, for example, on the one side, and Italy on the other. While the former country shows about 12% (offenses tried on indictment) and

23% (offenses tried summarily) of women among those convicted, the figures are 5 to 6% (assizes) and about 9% (corr. trib.) in the latter country. This difference shows that the direction in which the principal reason for woman's small part in crime must be sought, is in her social position. This differs less from that of the men in England than in Italy. However, there are figures much more significant than those I have just cited. Between 1893 and 1899 the percentage of convicts in prison in Scotland was between 36 and 37. In Denmark from 1876 to 1885 about 26% of the convicts were women. It is an incontestable fact that Denmark and Scotland are countries where the social position of women approaches most closely that of men. Let us set in opposition to this now a country like Algeria where the life of women is entirely different. It appears that there between 1881 and 1900 3% of those arraigned before the assizes were women, and 4% of those arraigned before the correctional tribunals.

An examination of the criminality of women in the different parts of the same country, Germany for example, shows that the highest figures for female criminality are furnished by the great cities and the countries most developed economically.

As regards England, Morrison says that of misdemeanors 25% are committed by women in London (Metropolitan Police District), and 33% in Manchester; while women commit only 10% of the misdemeanors in Surrey, and about 14% in Lancashire. The high percentages come then in the places where the social position of woman is most nearly equal to that of man.

        ✿   ✿   ✿

It must be conceded that the figures given do not contribute much to the support of the thesis that it is especially the social position of women which is the cause of their being less criminal. This position has been modified during the years to which the figures given refer. Women participate much more than formerly in the whole economic and social life. One would accordingly naturally look for a great increase in the criminality of women. Nevertheless these figures cannot, it seems to me, be used to refute the thesis in question, for the following reasons:

In the first place the figures given cover a short period only. They do not show very much, therefore; for, notwithstanding the continual increase of the importance of the rôle of woman in the economic life, the modification of her position in the whole social life is not made so quickly that one can expect much of an increase in female criminality in the criminal statistics of the last few years.

In the second place, most of the figures give the ratio of the crimes of women to those of men; they do not then show whether the decrease in the percentage is due to a decrease in the criminality of women, or rather to an increase in that of men. This latter is the case, for example, in Germany.

In the third place the statistics at my disposal are not sufficiently detailed with regard to the movement of the criminality of women, so that it is impossible to tell whether there are changes in the qualitative character of the crimes even though its quantitative character remains about the same.

A very conclusive proof of the thesis that the social position of woman is what explains her lower criminality, is as follows: The difference in the manner of life of the two sexes decreases as we descend the social scale. If the social position of woman is then an important determinant of her lower criminality, the figures ought to show that the criminality of men differs more from that of women in the well-to-do classes than in classes less privileged. Now the figures already given . . . upon the intellectual development of criminals confirm our hypothesis completely. Just so the tables upon the financial situation of criminals . . . ; in Austria, for example, 0.2% of the women convicted in 1899 came from the well-to-do classes, and 0.4% of the men. There were no well-to-do women at all among those convicted of the graver crimes. Just so again, in the table of Prussian recidivists the women form 4% of the well-to-do convicts and 14% of the poor convicts.

Finally the figures for the influence of marriage upon criminality show . . . that the criminality of widows is very great. This proves that the smaller criminality of woman is not to be sought in innate qualities, but rather in the social environment. For widows are generally forced to come into contact with the economic and social life of the world more than other women.

We have still to explain how social position is a cause of a lower degree of criminality. As to economic offenses, it must be remarked that the small part that woman plays in the economic life has the result that the desire to be enriched at some one else's expense is less aroused in her than it is in man, and that the opportunity to accomplish the desire is presented to her less often than to him. As to crimes committed for vengeance etc., since women live more retired lives they enter less quickly into conflict with others, and hence are less in danger of committing such crimes. Then the fact that women are less addicted to alcohol must be taken into account. The almost wholly negligible participation of women in political life explains why they are almost never guilty of political crimes, a kind of crime rare enough in any case.

After the long detour that we have made (in order to comprehend what follows), we come now at last to the subject which especially concerns us in this section, the influence of the economic and social life upon the social sentiments of women.

It results from this examination that, on the one hand, women feel generally less than men the direct harmful influences of the present economic system, and those of alcoholism; that the influence, very significant for criminality, of the environment in which she passes her youth, acts as strongly upon her as upon man; and that militarism has no influence upon her, nor has prostitution itself upon the majority of the sex.

Then woman has lived for ages in a state of oppression injurious to the development of the social instincts, which forces her to have recourse to lying and hypocrisy, those two defensive weapons of the oppressed. Just so also her retired life has been an obstacle to the development of her feeling of solidarity with reference to persons outside of the family.

In looking the whole field over I see nothing to justify the opinion that the less criminal character of women indicates a higher morality, whether innate or acquired. The consequences of her manner of life, in so far as they are harmful to the formation of character, are probably counterbalanced by those which are favorable. Her smaller criminality is like the health of a hothouse plant; it is due not to innate qualities, but to the hothouse which protects it from harmful influences. If the life of women were like that of men their criminality would hardly differ at all as to quantity, though perhaps somewhat as to quality.

e. The family. Here we have to take up the question of how far the family in which the criminal has been raised has contributed to make him such. It will be well to begin with some theoretical observations upon the question, what is the effect of moral education upon a child (in the larger sense of moral surroundings), and how far does this education in the end affect the adult?

It is unnecessary for us to tarry long upon this. The facts which we shall cite below are more convincing than all the theoretical observations, and they show clearly how great this influence is. Nevertheless some brief observations are necessary. It is not far from the truth, it seems to me, to say that the power of moral education upon the character, and that of intellectual education upon the intelligence, are equal. The thesis has been maintained that the intellectual capacities of all men are equal, and that education is the sole cause of the great differences which exist. No reasonable person would maintain this theory; men differ enormously in their innate intellectual capacities; some have great intellectual power, others have very little, while between the two extremes is found the general average. What now is the rôle that education has to play?

Those who have small intellectual capacity naturally never become superior men, even if their education is the best possible; though by virtue of proper education they might become fairly useful. Those who have great intellectual capacity also need education (though less so than the run of mankind), for otherwise their faculties will remain dormant. Darwin would never have made his great discovery if he had been born and reared in the slums of a great city and had learned nothing (even supposing that, with his poor health, he had not succumbed to such an environment). His acquaintances would have doubtless thought him intelligent, but the scientific world would never have heard of him.

It must be much the same with the moral faculty. We are not born with moral precepts in our heads, but only with a greater or less predisposition to become moral. If this predisposition, even though it be very strong, is not cultivated, there is no question of morality.

The child, even more than the man, is an imitator, and responds to suggestion in everything, but especially in morals. If we put the question: how does it happen that there are honest persons? the answer must be: largely because in their youth they have become accustomed to be honest. In his "Descent of Man," Darwin says: . . . "Habit in the individual would . . . play a very important part in guiding the conduct of each member; for the social instinct, together with sympathy, is like any other instinct, greatly strengthened by habit, and so consequently would be obedience to the wishes and judgment of the community."

A great proportion of the whole number of criminals have become such through the evil example of those about them, or have been deliberately trained to crime. Even those who are endowed with great innate moral capacities cannot withdraw themselves from these influences.

＊　　　＊　　　＊

In consequence of what we have just said we may put two questions; first, do all those who are brought up in such an environment inevitably become criminals? Second, is there, then, no difference as to morality between two persons of whom one is born with a strong and the other with a weak moral disposition (supposing that both live in the same unfavorable moral environment)?

The answer to the first question must be that there may be sometimes those who succeed notwithstanding the very bad surroundings of their youth. . . . But such cases are very rare and prove nothing against the theory of environment, for it may readily happen that such persons fall in with a better environment (at school, for example) which puts them on the right track, if they have a strong moral disposition by nature.

To the second question the answer must be made that one endowed with a strong moral disposition, but raised in unfavorable surroundings, will perhaps become criminal, and yet need not be as bad as another with a weak moral disposition, raised in a like environment.

There are criminals and criminals. Anyone who has given himself the trouble of reading the biographies of great criminals knows that all have not been entirely corrupted. It is with morals as with intelligence; in unfavorable circumstances Darwin would not have become a genius, but even in such environment he would nevertheless have been recognized as intelligent; so a child with great moral capacity would not become an honest man when brought up in the company of thieves and assassins, but in his own circle would have been considered as a good boy.

Besides very bad environments there are the great mass of those that are neither the one thing nor the other, in which the children neither have bad examples, nor are, properly speaking, deserted, but in which, nevertheless, they do not receive an education positively good. What is the influence of such environments? They are absolutely insufficient for children with little moral disposition. These have need of a strong and well-taught guide, without which they run much danger of leaving, sooner or later, the straight path. It is evident that an education such as that in question, is insufficient for the great middle class. The future lot of these young people will depend especially upon the circumstances in which chance shall place them. The surroundings spoken of will be enough for those who have great moral capacities, in the sense not that a better environment would not have had a better effect upon them but in the sense that they are more susceptible to the good than to the evil influences and—except in rare circumstances—they will cause less trouble to their fellows.

Finally, how far does the effect of a good education extend? What can a good education do for a person born with weak social instincts? This is the well-known controversy. For no one denies that those who are endowed with strong social instincts, as well as those who have them only in moderation, and who constitute the great majority, do not become bad when they are brought up in a good environment.

It will perhaps be impossible to give a decisive answer to this question. For, since we cannot make experiments with living persons, we cannot get sure results. And then an education really good is so great a rarity that the number of cases where children with little moral disposition are excellently brought up is certainly very small.

We may consider it as certain that children not well endowed will never become very altruistic even if brought up under the best conditions imaginable. But on the other hand no one would doubt that a favorable environment would develop, however little, their weak social instincts (for no one is wholly without such instincts). For the moment we cannot decide how far this influence may extend.

After this introduction we come to the organization of education in present-day society. Before stating the facts we must sum up what has been said above. . . . The organization of our present social system charges the legitimate parents of the child with his support and education. Most authors who treat of the family wax so enthusiastic that they lose all critical sense. They note that there are parents who love their children, perform all their duties towards them, etc., and they wish to make themselves believe that this is the general rule. But the subject must be considered in cold blood. Certainly it would be ridiculous to deny the social importance of the family; we may even say without hesitation that without the family our present society could not exist. But all this would not be a reason for not seeing its defects.

Are there not many who are bad, even aside from criminals? Is not the majority of mankind made up of those weak in character? Are there not many alcoholics? Are there not persons who do not love their children at all? Are not the persons numerous who have little patience and tact to guide children, or who are lacking in other pedagogic qualities? Is it not true that nearly everyone is ignorant of psychological and pedagogical principles? And have not most men their whole time taken up with the struggle for existence, so that they are not able to concern themselves with the education of their children?

These are the questions that we must ask ourselves; and the answer to all of them is categorically; yes. And have not all these persons offspring? Most certainly. Then the results may be imagined. It will be of the highest importance to know how many children receive an education that is really good. I do not know of any statistics covering any very great number of children. But it will not be far from the truth to infer that the following figures are applicable, not simply to a limited number, but in general to all children. These figures are given by Ferriani:

To each 100 children between 8 and 12 years of age:

Good education		5
Education fair		10
”	superficial	20
”	partially neglected	17
”	entirely ”	42
”	bad	6
		100

One of the characteristics of our present education is that it makes children egoistic. It is to be expected. The organization of society obliges men to be egoistic, and "like father, like son." An apparent morality is the consequence. Children are taught that they ought to do or leave undone this or that, not because it is needful to help their fellows or not to injure them, but because it will be advantageous to them to act morally, or because otherwise they will be punished. It is unnecessary to say that, brought up in such a manner, the individual will not recoil from crime because of any moral restraint, when the opportunity presents itself of making a profit, or when the risk of being punished is not great.

As to education among *the well-to-do classes*, there it is especially egoistic. The children—speaking of course in a general way—are brought up with the idea that they must succeed, no matter how; the aim of life is presented to them as getting money and shining in the world. Such principles are incompatible with a really moral education, and the education of this class aims only at an apparent morality instead of a real one.

Whatever may be the defects of this education, it is at least an education; the children are watched, prevented from getting into bad society, etc. The consequence is that the children of the well-to-do almost never get into the courts. This sad monopoly is reserved for the children of the poor. This is not to say that the defects of education among the well-to-do classes are not among the causes of the criminality to be met with in the adults of these classes. When a poor devil appears in court it will often happen that his counsel in defending him will draw attention to the fact that the environment in which his client has grown up is one of the causes of his fall; but it does not often happen that the advocate makes a similar appeal when his client is from the well-to-do. It is generally believed that nothing is wanting in the moral education of one who has not known poverty, and has not been neglected; but this is a mistake. There can be no doubt that one of the factors of criminality among the bourgeoisie is bad education.

The figures of the following tables show that it is almost exclusively the children of the poor who are guilty of crime.

* * *

It is then the poorest classes that furnish the greatest number of juvenile criminals.

We come now to education among the *proletariat*. Here we meet first, insufficiency of the pecuniary means which education requires; second, bad housing conditions, which oblige the children to pass a great part of the day in the street; third, the total absence of pedagogical ideas; fourth, the absence during the greater part of the day of the father of the family, and in many cases even of the mother. The number of married women who work away from home is continually increasing. In 1882 there were in Germany, for example, 507,784 married working-women, and by 1895 this figure had risen to 807,172—an increase of 299,388 (59%) in 13 years. In 1882 17.3% of the working-women were married; in 1895 21.5%. There are no official figures but Braun calculates that in Germany there are 500,000 children under 14 years of age, whose mothers are working-women. In Austria 44.6% of the working-women are married, and in France 20.6%. We have seen above . . . that juvenile criminality is increasing. This is explained in part by the increase in the labor of married women, from which it results that an increasing number of children are brought up without the proper care.

Among the working classes there is no question of education properly speaking. We can consider the children as fortunate if their parents do not set them a bad example, are not continually engaging in disputes, and are not given to alcohol. It is plain that all this does not make up a proper education; and yet how many children there are who do not have even so much of an education as this!

In the *lower proletariat* the situation is naturally worse. Not only is there a total lack of care and surveillance, but children are even brought up to crime.

Up to this point we have supposed the parents to be living. From the present organization of society it follows that the condition of the children of the poor becomes very bad as soon as the parents or even one of them dies. Often private or public charity intervenes, but generally the community does nothing for the orphan.

As a last consequence of the present system it must be noted that children born of illegitimate unions are in a still more precarious situation, since it is only the mother who has to protect them.

The community (in this case the state) concerns itself little with the education of children; it makes education compulsory (at least in some countries) and deprives parents of the charge of their children when they neglect them too much (this again in some countries only).

Now we come to the facts. They prove that the surroundings in which many children live are an important factor in the etiology of crime. The figures at my disposal are not as numerous as I could wish, but official statistics are not yet as full as is desirable for sociological purposes.

In reading the statistics which follow we must not lose sight of the fact that when it is stated that a certain percentage of children were brought up in a bad environment, it does not follow that all the others had a good education. The figures record only the very grave cases, as, for example, where the parents have been convicted, or the children entirely abandoned, etc. It is easier to prove, in making an investigation into the condition of a family, that the children do not receive a good education than it is to prove the contrary.

※   ※   ※

If the environment in which the young criminals have lived is the cause of their fall, a considerable portion of them ought to return to the right way as a result of the education given in the schools in question. If this is not the case with all, this proves nothing against the influence of environment, for the impressions received by the child in the surroundings in which he has lived before his conviction are too strong to be effaced by a comparatively brief stay in an educational institution (even if these reform-schools were perfect). Finally, after they are set at liberty environment may once more contribute to recidivism.

※   ※   ※

Finally it must be mentioned that 16.2% of 1,714 in the detention prison had alcoholic parents.

We are now at the end of our statistical data and also of our observations upon the environment in which criminals are brought up; for it seems to me superfluous to make further comments: the great influence of environment is indubitable.

Tomel and Rollet close their work "Enfants en prison" with these words, which I make my own, and which are as applicable to adult as to juvenile criminals: "Has society done everything that it ought to spare children the prison? We believe that with ourselves [the reader] will answer, 'No!' Each child to whom we refuse protection will become a delinquent. It is a wolf that we are preparing for the sheep-fold. If tomorrow he makes his fellows pay his own arrears of injustice, if he steals, if he kills, he will not say, 'I commit a crime'; he will say, 'I make reprisals.'"

f. Prostitution. Prostitution has a special importance for the etiology of sexual offenses and of procuration. However, it is not with this that we are concerned at present, but with the correlation between prostitution and criminality in general, in the sense, that is, that prostitution has a demoralizing effect upon the women who practice it and upon the men who have intercourse with them.

Let us begin with the effect upon the prostitutes themselves. And as with all observations upon the relation between certain social phenomena and criminality, these must be preceded by statistical data.

How large a quota do prostitutes contribute to crime? This is a hard question to answer, because, first, most criminal statistics make no mention of the occupation of prostitute; second, when the statistics do mention prostitution they do not give the real truth, since the facts will often be concealed by the woman interested; third, the extent of prostitution is almost unknown, so that it is impossible to make the necessary calculations.

❈   ❈   ❈

What data I have been able to secure do not prove—but render exceedingly probable—the assertion that prostitutes show a high degree of criminality. In my opinion this phenomenon is to be explained as follows.

First. From its nature the profession opens a vast field for committing economic offenses.

Second. Prostitution has a very demoralizing effect upon those that practice it. Those who have not sufficiently taken account of the real causes of prostitution consider this a confusing of cause and effect, and believe that it is the demoralization which causes prostitution. In reasoning thus they forget that part of the prostitutes are forced by poverty to take up this profession, and that in such cases there is no need of supposing demoralization. Whatever may be the case with regard to the rest, the profession would increase the demoralization already existing.

All the authors who have taken up the question are agreed that this is really the case. It is impossible to imagine a more degrading situation than that of a prostitute. A woman who is continually forced to act in opposition to her feelings, who is obliged to enter into intimate relations with the first comer however abject he may be, who has become unaccustomed to all work, and who is despised, inevitably loses all respect for herself and falls lower and lower.

A second bond of connection between criminality and prostitution is that it makes possible a category of persons who constitute a permanent danger to society, namely the "protectors." The unregistered prostitutes need a man who will look after them, and to whom they may attach themselves in their forlorn condition. In exchange for this protection the prostitute gives up a large part of her earnings. In examining the biographies of great criminals we see that a large number of them have belonged to this category. It is evident that only demoralized persons can lead such a life, but that this life in its turn increases their demoralization.

In the third place, prostitution has a demoralizing effect upon the men who come into contact with the prostitutes. We cannot lay it to chance that it is shown in many criminal procedures that guilty persons have had relations with the world of prostitution. This world includes only a relatively small number of persons; but the men who frequent it are numerous, and the demoralization which ensues is prejudicial to society. This demoralization is easily explained, as Dr. Lux shows in his "Sozialpolitisches Handbuch," in these words: "The venality of the delights of love debases the pleasure; the man learns to see in woman only a means of satisfying his lust; all higher regard for woman is lost to him, his thoughts become frivolous and cynical, his character continually more vulgar. Whoever has an opportunity to come to know the young men of the large cities, must, unless he is already tainted with their opinions himself, be shocked at the brutality and coarseness of their thought and speech. The whole conversational material of our gilded youth consists of filth and obscenities; they boast of things that a decent man would blush to be charged with. The young man is demoralized and depraved by association with prostitutes, of whose standard of morality he must beware lest he stifle in it every nobler feeling."

g. *Alcoholism*. Here we have to take up but a single one of the ways in which alcoholism is connected with criminality. For while acute alcohol-poisoning enters into the etiology of sexual offenses and those committed in revenge, etc., it has almost no relation to the largest of the classes, namely economic crimes. Acute alcoholism, therefore, has no place among our general observations. With chronic alcoholism it is otherwise; for the man who is subject to this undergoes a general demoralization by which he is predisposed to crime even when he is not drunk. The manner in which demoralization takes place is not a question within the province of sociology; it is sufficient for us that this consequence of chronic alcoholism is universally recognized.

To show the influence of chronic alcoholism upon criminality we can use only the direct statistical method; that is to say, we must find the number of chronic alcoholics among criminals, and then place beside this the number among the non-criminal population, in order that we may compare them. If the latter figures are lacking, a comparison is impossible. However, as we shall see, the percentage of chronic alcoholics is so great among the criminals, that we can affirm that among the non-criminals the percentage is very small. Consequently the influence of chronic alcoholism, whether greater or less, is indubitably proved.

❊   ❊   ❊

The data given above show sufficiently, it seems to me, what the relation is between chronic alcoholism and criminality. Notwithstanding their divergences the percentages in the different countries are generally very high, and in every case much higher than among the non-criminal population. The danger that these statistics are based upon inaccurate data is not great, since the culprit has every reason to pretend that his act has been committed in a state of intoxication, in order that he may be less severely punished, and not that he is a chronic alcoholic.

There still remains the question as to what is the degree of influence which chronic alcoholism has upon crime. We should be exaggerating if we were to declare (as is sometimes done by total abstainers) that whenever a criminal is an habitual alcoholic, alcoholism is one of the principal causes of his crime. It is evident that in many cases it is only an accidental phenomenon. Nevertheless, the figures given above agree with the thesis that chronic alcoholism is a demoralizing agent and as such belongs to the etiology of crime. Its influence naturally cannot be exactly expressed in figures.

h. Militarism. Although the influence of militarism upon criminality may not be an important factor in comparison with some others, it is still necessary to speak of it here briefly, and under two heads: its influence in time of peace, and its influence in time of war.

First, the influence of militarism in time of peace. The army is recruited in great part among those who do not volunteer, in other words among persons who have not the least taste for the military life and only serve for fear of incurring severe penalties. Then a great number of the volunteers have become soldiers only from necessity, because they could not find a place for themselves anywhere else. Finally one class of volunteers have enlisted very young, for a long term of service, perhaps at the instance of their parents, or drawn by the brilliant uniform, or other means of advertising peculiar to the army. It is unnecessary to add that for the last two classes the military service is often a deception, which makes them regret having engaged in it.

The first source of demoralization in an army is to be found in its composition. When you bring together a number of men, uneducated for the most part, with nothing to unite them but constraint, and when there are already certain bad elements among them, the demoralizing influence makes itself felt at once. No moral bond unites these men, but on the contrary a vague irritation begins to spread. And this demoralization is not counteracted by that great moral force, work; a great part of the time among the soldiers is passed in forced idleness, and the rest in learning things in which they have little interest, if indeed they do not feel an aversion to them.

It is naturally only by a discipline of iron that order can be maintained and the recruits taught their trade. As soon as a man is debased by excessive discipline to the rôle of a machine, his moral qualities deteriorate; the state of things thus created brings it about that the great power given to superiors often degenerates into a thirst for domination, and renders the subordinates servile, and yet of the opinion that anything is right for them so long as they are not found out.

Since most soldiers are only under arms for a short time, the consequences named are not of great importance for them, but those consequences nevertheless exist for the professional soldier. The best known set of statistics upon the criminality among soldiers is that of Hausner, who shows that it is 25 times as great among soldiers as the criminality of civilians. These figures, however, have little value, because among the civilians are counted not simply the men of military age, but the whole population. Further, a statistical comparison of military and civil criminality will always meet with great difficulties, for, first, there are offenses of which only soldiers can be guilty; second, the number of the soldiers is not constant even in any one year. Although we cannot, therefore, express in figures the harmful influences of militarism, it exists, nevertheless. But even if we had the figures and they were to show—supposing a most improbable case—that criminality was no greater among soldiers than in civil life, even this would not contradict the evil influence of military life, since repression and the fear of punishment are greater among soldiers than among civilians, and abject poverty, one of the powerful factors in economic criminality, is totally lacking in the army.

The question may be raised as to whether the disadvantages spoken of above are inseparable from every form of organization of the army. The answer must be that this is the case in part only. The harmful consequences will partially disappear when the army is adapted to the democratic spirit, and the service remains limited to the time strictly necessary to make a good soldier; but the fact that the great mass of which the army is composed has no sympathy with its aim and end but remains in service only by constraint, will continue to exist. This latter circumstance will disappear only in the country where the army is exclusively for the purposes of defense, to repulse an enemy that wishes to destroy democratic institutions.

We come now to the influence of war itself. That which, at ordinary times, is one of the gravest crimes, homicide, is commanded in war; ravages and burnings are the order of the day. It is inevitable that those who are driven to commit such acts, lose little by little their respect for the lives and property of their fellows. War arouses a spirit of violence, not only in those who take part in it, but in the whole population.

Happily wars are neither so numerous nor so long continued as formerly, so that the consequences have no longer so wide a scope.

Statistical research into the influence of war upon criminality is very difficult, for criminality diminishes in time of war in an abnormal fashion, first, because a great part of the male population of the age most disposed to crime is under arms; second, the repression of crime being less vigorous makes the degree of criminality appear smaller than it really is, which explains why the figures for the criminality of women and juveniles are less.

We often hear that war has also a good moral influence, since the whole nation is then animated with a single ideal. This is true only in the very rare cases where a war is really popular, in place of being the means of procuring material profits for a small minority, while the great majority remain indifferent. It goes without saying that even in these exceptional cases, the harmful consequences to the participants still remain.

We have examined the tendencies of the present economic system and all its consequences. Before concluding we must treat of the effect of

i. The penalty. The present codes give prominence to three kinds of penalties: fines, different kinds of imprisonment, and capital punishment. We naturally do not have to say anything of the first of these, since there can be no question raised as to its effect upon the person upon whom the fine is laid. All that we can say is that this penalty fails of its object since no account is taken of the financial condition of the person sentenced to it, and it follows that while the punishment involved is only trifling for the rich, it constitutes a heavy burden for the poor. Often a fine for a poor man who cannot pay is simply a sentence for a short imprisonment.

The death penalty also naturally is outside of our present discussion. I would simply observe that among the numerous arguments against this penalty it must be noted that it has no intimidating effect upon those who are present, as one would suppose, but on the contrary a demoralizing influence; besides which the attention of the ignorant class is drawn to the crime and the perpetrator of it. Those who are condemned to death have almost all been present at executions. Out of a total of 511 of whom we have information, there were only 15 (about 3%) who had never witnessed an execution.

In investigating the influence of punishment upon morality it is imprisonment alone, therefore, which must be taken into consideration, so much the more since even in the case of minor crimes it is almost always inflicted, while capital punishment is either altogether abolished, as in some countries, or else rarely pronounced and still more rarely executed.

＊　　＊　　＊

The imperfection of the present mode of combating crime is shown even by the evidence of the statistics we have given. It would be hard to imagine a more complete fiasco; in place of a decrease there has been an increase in recidivism; in place of making men better, the prison makes them worse.

Here is in brief the explanation of the fact. As we have already observed above in treating of the definition of crime, one of the important elements in the present system of punishment consists, for many people, in the desire to satisfy their revengeful feelings excited by the crime. Those who realize that the punishment must be especially aimed at the improvement of the criminal form only a small minority. The present forms of punishment and the manner in which they are inflicted are little if at all in accord with this latter point of view. At present the penalty is not much more than an evil inflicted upon the criminal to satisfy the vengeance of a great part of mankind, and at the same time to make it impossible for the criminal to do harm, either for a time or else forever, and finally to terrify him and other men into not committing crimes. *So long as punishment has this characteristic, so long as it does not aim at the improvement of the criminal, so long will it fail to effect a decrease in crime, but will rather bring an increase, as the facts prove.* No one, not even the most dangerous criminal is morally improved in the slightest degree by vengeance wreaked upon him. Vengeance engenders only vengeance and no other feeling. We can expect to see good results from punishment only if the criminal, from the manner in which he is treated, perceives that those who have him in charge wish him well, are trying to improve him, and that his act was wicked and intolerable.

There are two types of imprisonment; imprisonment in common, and in separate cells. It is very easy to understand that a term of imprisonment served in common has disastrous consequences for the prisoner. It is because of this system that the prison has had the name of a school of crime, which would be a good joke if the facts were less serious. All kinds of criminals, young and old, those sentenced for minor offenses, and those guilty of grave crimes, criminals against property and criminals against persons, all find themselves massed together, so that instead of leaving prison bettered, almost every one leaves it worse that he went in. No work is done, or at least only stupefying labors; a real trade is neither practiced nor learned.

The disadvantages of this system have led to the cellular plan by which the contagious influences of the prison are gotten rid of. Much was hoped for from the change, but the statistics of recidivism show the hope to have been ill-founded; separate confinement improves the prisoner no more than the older type. This fact is not difficult to explain. Starting from the false theory that man has a free will, the non-determinists have believed, and unhappily still believe, that the criminal left to himself and to his own reflections will repent. As Sacker in "Der Rückfall" judiciously remarks, the criminal must not be left to his thoughts —if he has any—but must be given new ideas. It is unnecessary to remark that it is not life in a cell that will give them to him.

Man is a social being; without life among his fellows he is like an animal out of its element. How can he become better if he lives alone. The cell stupefies him, isolation and monotony make him a machine, which later will not be fit for a free life. I do not know a better description of the consequences of separate confinement than that given by the competent author of "Pictures and Problems from London Police Courts," Th. Holmes. He says: "How is it that a man's facial expression changes during a long detention? How is it that his voice becomes hard and unnatural? How is it that his eyes become shifty, cunning, and wild? It is no fault of the prison officials; they cannot help these things; from the governor downward they are not to blame. It is not because of hard work. From conversation with, and knowledge of, such men, I gather that some of them at any rate would be thankful for more work. It is the system that does it, the long-continued, soul-and-mind-destroying monotony, the long, silent nights in which for hours men lie awake thinking, thinking, thinking, driven in upon themselves and to be their own selves' only companion. No interchange of ideas is possible, no sound of human voices comes to call forth their own, and their own vocal organs rust. Nor does returning day bring change, nothing but the same duties, performed in the same way, at the same hour, and the same food, in the same quantities, served in the same demoralizing way. They become strangers to the usages of civilized society, and devour their food even as the beasts, but not with the wild beast's relish. To the use of knife and fork they become strangers; to a knowledge of their own lineaments they become strangers; to high thoughts, amiable words, courtesy, love of truth, and all that makes a man become strangers, for these virtues cannot dwell with senseless monotony. But if these things die of atrophy, other but less desirable qualities are developed. A low cunning takes their place; the wits are sharpened to deceive or to gain small ends; hypocrisy is developed, and men come out of prison hating it, loathing it, but less fitted to perform the duties of life than when they entered it."

Read further the opinion of Dostoievsky: "I am firmly convinced that the boasted cellular system pursues but a false, if specious, aim. It sucks the vital power out of a man, enervates his mind, weakens and cows him, and finally presents the desiccated mummy of a man made half mad, as a picture of reformation and repentance."

It would be possible to fill these pages with the well-supported opinions of those who regard the cellular system as "an aberration of the 19th century" (Ferri).

To sum up, then, we come to the conclusion that the system of imprisonment is not in a condition to arrest the tide of criminality, but further that it is even one of the causes of the increase of crime, since it makes the prisoners still worse. It may be that in consequence of what I have just said the reader will remark that there is no other expedient possible than imprisonment, whether in common or cellular. Although the question of the treatment of the criminal as it ought to be is not one of those with which we are at present occupied, I shall nevertheless say a few words on the subject.

It is possible to practice a third system, which takes its origin from the idea that the crime does not proceed from the free will, but from causes which it will be necessary to try to remove, in place of inflicting a useless punishment. It is to the credit of the State of New York that it should be the first to put in practice this sort of a system of combating crime (in the Elmira Reformatory). An effort is made to make a man of the criminal, to turn him into a strong and sound individual; he is taught a trade, his mind is elevated, his feeling of honor revived; in short, everything is done that is necessary to stimulate the development of what is human in the man. And the results prove that those who are following this method are surely on the right road.

There is only one objection to this system; that many persons who have not committed crime lead a life which in various ways is worse than that of the criminals so treated. However, this very sound objection does not condemn the system, but rather the present organization of society, which obliges a great number of persons to drag out a miserable existence. The question of crime and the social question are inseparable; he who examines the first without the second will not do much toward solving it.

j. Imitation. Before concluding we must give our attention to one more factor: imitation. We have already pointed this out in speaking of the moral education of the young, but it is also of importance with adults . . . , though not to so great an extent. When society shows very egoistic tendencies imitation strengthens these considerably; when we see persons with whom we have to do, always acting in an egoistic manner, our anti-egoistic forces weaken little by little and we end by doing as the others do. In the crime of mobs imitation plays an important part.

The proofs to support the power of imitation in the etiology of crime are to be found in the biographies of most great criminals; bad example plays generally a preponderant rôle in the drama of life.

*   *   *

A second proof of the influence of the contagion of crime is found in the fact that the criminality in the cities, where people come more into contact with each other, is in general greater than that in the country. Although it is evident that we cannot impute this exclusively to imitation (it is due, among other things, in part to the great differences of fortune found in the cities), it still plays an important part.

*   *   *

An examination of the statistics given shows that except for a few offenses the cities are more criminal than the country.

However, it must not be forgotten that the cities have proportionately a greater number of inhabitants at the age at which there is the greatest tendency to crime, and that the figures therefore give the criminality of the cities as a little greater than it is. On the other hand there is a greater proportion of crimes that are not prosecuted, or whose authors remain undiscovered. The English statistics, which do not speak of the persons arraigned or convicted, but of the crimes known to the police, are better in this regard.

It is unnecessary to treat more fully of the rôle of imitation in the etiology of crime; no one will deny it. As I have already noted . . . in my criticism of the theory of Tarde, imitation is not an independent factor, but dependent upon others. In our present society, with its pronounced egoistic tendencies, imitation strengthens these, as it would strengthen the altruistic tendencies produced by another form of society. Man does not imitate that which is egoistic simply, but also that which is altruistic. It is only as a consequence of the predominance of egoism in our present society that the error is made of supposing the effect of imitation to be necessarily evil.

k. Conclusions. In recapitulating now the egoistic tendencies of the present economic system and of its consequences, we see clearly that they are very strong. Because of these tendencies the social instinct of man is not greatly developed; they have weakened the moral force in man which combats the inclination towards egoistic acts, and hence towards the crimes which are one form of these acts. To mention only the most important things, in a society in which, as in ours, the economic interests of all are in eternal conflict among themselves, compassion for the misfortunes of others inevitably becomes blunted, and a great part of morality consequently disappears. The slight value that is attached to the opinion of others is also a consequence of the strife of economic interests, for we can be responsive to that opinion only when we do not see adversaries in our fellows.

The fluctuations of the mind of the person in whom the criminal idea is born may be compared with the oscillations of a balance; and it is upon sociology that must devolve the task of examining the forces which throw a weight on one side or the other. When the organization of society influences men in an altruistic way there is then a considerable force which can prevent the balance from inclining towards the egoistic side. In our present society, the organization of which does not exert an altruistic influence, this force is very weak, or does not exist at all. Since, however, in every society, man must abstain from a number of egoistic acts, substitutes have been devised to take the place of the weak or wanting social sentiments. The hope of reward (whether terrestrial or celestial) and the fear of being punished (whether by man or God) are charged with the duty of keeping men in order. As believers themselves know very well, most men are not very responsive to divine rewards and punishments—heaven and hell are too far off. Is it not believers who are the strongest partisans of rewards and punishments here below for human acts? However, this expedient is only a very insufficient one. We know too well that the rewards are often lacking, and the punishments as well. This is why many persons take the risk of committing the crime they have planned.

The present environment exercises an egoistic influence upon all men. We all participate, for example, in exchange, which, as we have seen, is a great egoistic factor; and other similar factors could be named that act upon all. On the other hand there are other egoistic factors which exercise their influence only upon some of us.

Let us compare two totally different environments in which an individual grows up. Let us place him first in the slums of a great city; his father is alcoholic, his mother a prostitute; he has never attended school, passing his time in vagabondage up to the day when, still young, he has been committed to prison, where his education in crime is completed. Now let us suppose this same individual to have grown up in a healthy environment, where neither poverty nor extreme riches exercised their pernicious influence. He has been brought up by rational and loving parents, his mind has been developed, he has found later a good career, in which the greed of gold has not been aroused in him. We shall then have before us two extremes, between which a great many degrees are to be found. The environment is a very important cause of the great diversity among men. However, it is not the only one; we still must give our attention for a moment to:

D. Individual Differences

Men differ in height, in strength, in weight, in intellectual capacity, in everything, in short. Apparently no regularity is to be seen in their diversity. If, for example, we look at a crowd with reference to the heights of the individuals composing it, there seems to be no regularity about them.

*   *   *

The irregularity is [however] only apparent; there is regularity in this sense, that the persons of average height predominate very greatly in number, and that the very short and very tall persons form minorities. This regularity in the individual differences, discovered by Quetelet, has been recognized as a universal law, applicable to everything living. The scientist named has demonstrated this not only for the height of the human body, but also for its weight, strength, quickness, etc.

Galton has proved the existence of this law for the intellectual capacity of man, and a number of other scientists have done the same for the animal and vegetable kingdoms. Hence, "uniformity in variability" for all living nature must be considered as a universal law.

The same thing must be true for men's moral qualities. In ranking any number of persons according to the intensity of their innate social sentiments (supposing it were possible to apply a measure to these), we should find that here also the law in question held good; with the great majority the social sentiments would have only a moderate intensity, while there would be one small minority in which they would be weak, and another in which they would be very strong. We have no need to revert to the influence of the environment, for we have seen that it gives to all an egoistic or altruistic impulse, differing naturally according to the individual. Supposing that the environment were the same for all, there would still be great differences between men as to the intensity of their social sentiments.

What is now the importance of this fact for the etiology of crime? In my opinion, the answer to this question will not be different from those which have been given to analogous questions when we were treating of the etiology of prostitution and alcoholism . . . , namely, that in every society, everywhere and always, an individual, according as his social sentiments are weaker or stronger than another's, runs more or less risk than [the other] of becoming a criminal, supposing the environment of the two to be the same in effect. . . . This point is of great importance for anyone who is investigating why the first falls into crime and not the latter. But it has little weight for criminal sociology, which concerns itself, not with definite persons, but only with general social facts.

The evidence that individuals differ quantitatively always and everywhere does not give the explanation of the problems whose solution sociology seeks, although they must be taken into account. *The task that is incumbent upon it is to explain why individuals who, as a consequence of their innate qualities, run more danger than others of becoming criminals, actually become so.* He who is born with weak social instincts runs more *danger* of becoming a criminal. But the *certainty* that he will become such does not exist—that depends upon the environment.

To sum up; I am of the opinion that individual differences are of great importance for one who is studying an individual by himself, but that they do not belong to the domain of the etiology of criminality.

E. The Classification of Crime

Before proceeding to the treatment of crimes separately, it is necessary to divide them into some main groups. It is a grave error (committed, however, by many criminologists) not to take account of the very different nature of crimes, if one is concerned with their etiology. It is, to be sure, permissible to treat conjointly moral forces which may prevent the execution of criminal ideas and which apply to all crimes. I have done so in the preceding pages. But we cannot treat the origin of the criminal idea itself in this same way. There are criminals and criminals. There are enormous differences between a professional thief, and a man who has been guilty of assault and battery in a state of intoxication, just as there are between a ravisher and a political criminal. And anyone who does not take account of these diffrences must necessarily limit himself to certain generalities.

I propose to treat of crimes divided into four categories in accordance with the motives which led their authors to commit them. Three of these categories form quite definite units, while the fourth is more heterogeneous.

The first is composed of crimes that have an economic aim (economic crimes). The greater part of the so-called crimes against property, such as theft, embezzlement, etc., belong to this category, but not all, for malicious mischief, for example, is generally dictated by a desire for vengeance. On the other hand some crimes against the person, like procuration, the object of which is economic and not sexual, belong here. As for crimes against the state, we must add counterfeiting to this category. Then there are other crimes that may be committed either for economic or non-economic reasons; for example, murder (for the purpose of robbery or for revenge), perjury (for the profit of winning a civil suit, or to prevent the conviction of a friend), arson (to get the insurance money, or for revenge), etc.

It may be urged here that, notwithstanding the similarity of their motives the crimes of any class still present many differences. This is true in part, and I have accordingly subdivided them. But on the other hand these differences are not very great *from the standpoint of criminal sociology*. For the jurist the difference between counterfeiting bank-notes, burning a house to get the insurance, and procuration is very important; but for sociology it is much less so. A man who knows how to make counterfeit bank-notes, will commit this crime, whenever he wishes for any reason to enrich himself in a dishonest fashion, but he will become neither an incendiary nor a procurer. A former prostitute, on the contrary, will not think of making bank-notes, but will become a procuress. The kind of economic crime committed by the person who has a mind to commit such a crime, depends principally upon chance (occupation, etc.).

The second category includes sexual crimes, and the fourth political crimes—two categories quite distinct therefore.

The other misdemeanors and crimes form the third category, and are more or less heterogeneous. The principal motive of these crimes is vengeance. Among them are insults, malicious mischief, assaults, homicide, etc. Other motives are: the fear of shame (infanticide, which, however, may also be committed for economic reasons); then fear of falling into the hands of justice (perjury, rebellion); and some others besides.

Finally, to give a picture of the quantitative proportions of the principal crimes, I add here some figures upon criminality in some of the countries of Europe. These figures may at the same time serve to show to those who are not acquainted with criminal statistics, how regular a course crime has from one year to another.

It is crimes of vengeance, therefore, which form the largest group, then come economic crimes, and then sexual and political crimes, both with low figures. If we do not count the very minor offense of insult in the third group, the first and third groups will be nearly of the same size. There are, then, almost no political crimes in England. As in Germany, sexual crimes are very rare, and it is the economic crimes and those committed out of revenge, etc., that are the most important. The latter preponderate even more in England than in Germany.

* * *

Finally, it must not be forgotten that certain crimes of a different kind (leze majesty and malicious mischief, for example) are sometimes committed simply that the author of them may get himself imprisoned, and hence should be classed as economic crimes.

We have now reached the question: how close a connection have the different crimes with economic conditions? We shall give only a detailed sketch of the subject; to treat it more fully would require extensive monographs. We shall limit ourselves to indicating the general lines.

II
Economic Crimes

It is necessary to divide these crimes into separate groups. Notwithstanding their partial similarity they differ too much among themselves to be treated together. I propose to speak of them under the four following heads: A. Vagrancy and mendicity; B. Theft, and analogous crimes; C. Robbery, homicide for economic reasons, etc. (that is to say, economic crimes committed with violence or directed against life); D. Fraudulent bankruptcy, adulteration of food, etc. (that is to say, economic crimes committed almost exclusively by the bourgeoisie, while those of the first three categories are committted almost exclusively by the poor). Some crimes, like that of embezzlement, belong to the second class as well as to the fourth (for example, a workman's making off with a bicycle loaned to him, and the embezzlement of deposits by a bank director).

It seems to me unnecessary to explain this division. It creates four fairly distinct groups, which contain all the economic crimes. However, I must point out why I treat vagrancy and mendicity in this way, while both are generally regarded not as misdemeanors but as contraventions. Properly speaking they ought not, therefore, to appear in a work on criminality, but the following are the reasons why they nevertheless find a place here; first they are the most important and the most common contraventions; second there is a very close relation between vagrancy on the one hand, and criminality on the other.

*   *   *

A. Vagrancy and Mendicity

In examining the etiology of these contraventions, we perceive that different causes lead to them. We shall treat them successively and endeavor to find their relation to the economic life.

First. As a first cause of vagrancy and mendicity is the fact that under capitalism there are always workmen who cannot sell their labor. The number of these persons increases greatly at the time of a crisis. When the men out of work have no resource in their family and no longer receive aid from their union, they are obliged to go from place to place looking for employment, and if they do not succeed in finding it must have recourse to begging in order not to die of hunger. Statistics furnish the proof that the army of vagrants and mendicants is in fact made up in part of the unemployed who, though they wish to, cannot find work.

In the first place, vagrancy and mendicity increase in winter (as in general all economic criminality does), when forced unemployment is at its height, and needs are most pressing, while they diminish in summer.

*   *   *

Another proof in support of the assertion that unemployment is a cause of mendicity and vagrancy, is to be found in the fact that the figures for vagrancy and mendicity rise considerably at the time of economic crises. The same phenomenon occurs more or less when the price of grain or bread goes up. Then those whose labor is only poorly paid must find some means of increasing their resources; and further when bread is dear less of other things can be bought, which brings about a decrease in production and consequently an increase in forced idleness.

        ✿   ✿   ✿

With some exceptions the curve of vagrancy rises and falls, then, pretty much as the economic situation grows worse or improves.

        ✿   ✿   ✿

I am of the opinion that these data show sufficiently that the increase or diminution of vagrancy and mendicity are regulated by the economic situation; in other words, that a great many persons become guilty of these contraventions not because they are not *willing* to work, but *entirely* as a consequence of an unfavorable economic environment. There are some exceptions to this rule. Above . . . I have shown that these exceptions do not weaken the general conclusion; the unfavorable influence of the economic depression may be neutralized by counter-determinants. It must further be remarked especially with regard to vagrancy and mendicity, that the application of the laws relative to these offenses is quite arbitrary, and it happens at the time of a crisis that the courts do not punish those who are guilty of them, whence it follows that the statistics do not give an accurate picture of the reality.

It is impossible to fix exactly how far the influence of economic depressions extends; in other words, we cannot determine the number of vagrants and mendicants who become such *directly* through forced idleness. When it is necessary to record a certain number of convictions for vagrancy and mendicity, although the economic conditions are most favorable, we shall not even then be able to say that this proves that the convictions fell only upon persons who could have found work, but did not wish it.

Under the present economic system unemployment is chronic, that is to say, it is present even in times of economic prosperity. Consequently it has not been proved that those who are convicted during these periods are necessarily lazy and do not want to work. The only figure that I have been able to find with regard to the importance of this cause of vagrancy and mendicity is this: that in Germany, out of a total of 200,000 mendicants, there are 80,000 (40%) who are really in search of work. This figure being only approximate, its significance is not great.

Before leaving the subject of this cause, we must say something with regard to the objection that the workers who, on account of a long period of unemployment, fall finally into vagrancy, are inferior to the average, generally do not know a trade, and are often addicted to alcohol; and that consequently in this case an individual factor plays a rôle beside the economic factor.

It is true that most of the vagrants and mendicants do not know a trade, nor are worth much as workmen. In his study Dr. Bonhoeffer says that 55.4% of the vagrants and mendicants examined by him had not learned a trade, or had learned it insufficiently. This author also shows (we shall return to this later) that a great proportion of these people are also physically inferior to the average. This inferiority is in part not the cause but the effect of the conditions under which they have been living (insufficient food, etc.), and in part congenital weakness.

However, supposing that each of these individuals knew a trade, supposing also that they are all robust and healthy and in a condition to work regularly, would there then be fewer persons without work than there are now? *The answer to this question must be negative.* Even if every workman knew a trade, this fact would not increase the demand for skilled workmen. At any given time the labor market demands a certain number of skilled workmen, and a certain other number of unskilled laborers; the number of unskilled laborers available has no influence. The same thing is true as to fitness for work; if all the workmen had the same energy, the same zeal, etc., this would not increase the demand for workmen; this demand is regulated by other factors.

In my opinion it cannot be a question of individual causes; individual differences explain partially who remain without work, and so become vagrants; but it is the economic system which causes the existence of persons without work. *Vagrancy and mendicity would be no less extensive even if all the workers knew a trade and were equal in zeal and energy.*

In the second place the world of vagrants and mendicants is composed of people too old to work, or more or less incapable of working, from physical or psychical causes, so that they are no longer employed.

❊   ❊   ❊

All that I have just said demonstrates sufficiently, I believe, that the cause named above plays a considerable rôle in the etiology of mendicity and vagrancy. It is still necessary to give an answer to the question: do all individuals who fall under the unfavorable conditions named under one and two, become vagrants or mendicants? It is evident that the answer must be negative. Three expedients offer themselves to one who has fallen into the blackest poverty: mendicity, theft, and suicide. It is partly chance (opportunity etc.), and partly the individual predisposition which fixes what anyone under the conditions named will become, whether a mendicant or a thief. Generally those who have still some intelligence and energy become thieves, the rest vagrants. The third expedient, suicide, also is frequently met with among the lower proletariat. Those who have recourse to it are either those who have known better conditions and find

that the miserable existence that mendicity procures is not worth
the trouble of living, or those who have lost all energy. Sometimes persons commit suicide to escape the shame of begging or
stealing. These have been called "the heroes of virtue"; but, considered from another point of view, they may also be called the
"victims of vice," the vice of others, of course. These have been
born with a very strong moral disposition and have lived in an
environment where this disposition has been developed. These
cases prove the degree of intensity that the social sentiments can
attain; they are stronger than the fundamental desire to live,
although those whom these "heroes" are unwilling to injure,
reject these sentiments, by abandoning their fellows who find
themselves in want.

Third. A third category of mendicants and vagrants is made
up of children and young people. Let us see what relation there
is between this fact and the economic and social environment.
All those who have taken up this subject are agreed that a great
proportion of the children are systematically taught to beg by
their parents. Whatever may be the cause for which the parents
act thus, these children are entirely the victims of the detestable
atmosphere in which they are forced to live. Brought up in a
wholesome environment they would become neither mendicants
nor vagrants.

Another part of the vagrant body is made up of children who
are either illegitimate or orphans, or deserted by their parents, or
forced by bad treatment to run away from home.

*   *   *

We must now speak of another kind of vagrant and mendicant,
those whom some criminologists have called born-vagabonds;
children who run away from home to meet with adventures and
to see something more than the neighborhood where they live.
It makes little difference to us here whence comes this desire;

everyone, especially every child, has it more or less (who is there who does not love to travel?) and there are those in whom it is very strong. "Who among us," say Tomel and Rollet, "at certain moments of existence, does not feel the desire to break with social conventions, or more simply, to break through the circle of his horizon, in order to depart in search of the unknown? Put money in the pocket of the tramp and you make a tourist. The sportsman and the delinquent are separated only by the thickness of some hundred-sou pieces."

These authors have hit the truth of the matter. Such children are called born-vagabonds, but then we meet thousands of born-vagabonds who have never become vagabonds in reality. The children who have a great love of adventure are found in all classes of society, but only those who come from among the poor become vagrants. It is in poverty then that we find the "causa efficiens"; the same inclination that brings poor children to prison, would perhaps lead them to a post of honor if they had lived in better surroundings. There are people of all kinds among criminals, and it cannot be denied that the majority of them are inferior in every way. But this does not apply to this class of little vagrants. Those who, as a consequence of years of experience, have a right to speak, are agreed that such children can be made useful members of society, if they are rationally guided. They are bold and energetic lads. Could it be believed that all the boys who, in 1889, came on foot to Paris from all parts of France to see the Eiffel tower (there were some of them under seven years of age) were not brave and energetic? Brought up in another environment they would have become sailors or explorers, or would have undertaken long journeys as tourists—while now they get into prison, to descend later lower and lower.

Fourth. Finally, the fourth category of vagrants and mendicants. This consists of those not included in the other three classes of people, who are physically in a condition to work and who have opportunity to do so, but are not willing to work. It is hard to determine with certainty how large a part of the army of vagrants and mendicants they make up. But it seems to me certain that the facts given above prove that they are not as numerous as some authors and many other people believe. Besides, how is it that the philanthropic institutions where everyone admitted has to work, are always full, if it is true that most vagrants are persons who are not willing to work?

The vagrants of this class are then lazy persons, unwilling to work, but living at the expense of others, and consequently parasites. It is with reason that many authors have blamed such persons (though, as Dr. Colajanni says, justice would require that we should include all do-nothings, and not the poor only). But this does not advance the cause of sociology; her task is to find the causes of the phenomenon.

It is incontestable that the zeal and energy, evidenced by modern peoples in their work, are not innate but acquired. All sound individuals have, not in the same measure, it is true, an innate tendency to exercise their muscles and their intellectual faculties, but without external causes this inclination does not go very far. The primitive peoples work no more than is necessary to provide for their very moderate needs. They find people laughable who work more than is strictly necessary. The enormous change which took place in the method of production little by little induced men to produce a greater and greater amount of work; on the one hand were the slaves, forced to labor hard, and on the other hand the property owners driven to work by the desire of profit. In our present society the case is almost the same; the great mass are forced to work by fear of poverty, the smaller number by the desire for gain. And then the great majority of men have been accustomed to work from infancy; much work is done from necessity, but much from habit, which causes a feeling of uneasiness when one cannot work.

The first reason why there are people who do not want to work, is that they have not been accustomed to it from childhood. In general children, like primitive people, who are analogous to them in many ways, show little zeal for work. It is necessary to train them for a fairly long time before they set themselves to work assiduously. What will all those children whose parents have neglected them, or who have even taught them to beg, turn into when they are grown up, if not into vagrants and mendicants? They have never learned any trade, have never become accustomed to work, have never found any pleasure in it, so that later in life they will never have any desire to do anything.

Part of those who have not been able to work for a long time go the same road; they lose the habit of working, become lazy, and in the end are not willing to do anything any more. These, to be sure, are the least diligent by nature, but that would not alone send them into vagrancy if they had always been able to find work.

However, there is still one more thing to be said about the circumstances which give rise to this class of individuals. In the first place, the long duration, the monotony, and the disagreeable features of the work of the proletariat, which, as a consequence is rather hated than loved. In the second place: the small wages of a large part of the workers, and the comparatively large amounts that clever beggars are able to secure.

❊   ❊   ❊

In some cases, then, it is more profitable, and in all cases more easy, not to work. In consequence of these facts we read very often that the public ought not to give to these idlers. But the public cannot distinguish this class of mendicants from the others. It is certainly true that professional mendicity would diminish if nothing were given to mendicants; but on the other hand the great misery among the other poor would be aggravated still more. And I venture to doubt whether the advantage thus gained on one side would counter-balance the disadvantage created on the other.

And these laments upon the subject of the stupidity of the public are generally accompanied by anathemas upon those who prefer the life of the parasite to work. No one would naturally be inclined to excuse these individuals. But it is necessary to look at the question from both sides. If these people are blamed, blame must be attached also to a state of society *in which honest labor is so poorly paid that begging is often more lucrative.* These individuals are cunning egoists and as long as society is organized as it is, they are right from their point of view. To be sure, they have no feeling of honor, they attach no value to the opinion of others, but the feeling of honor is not innate but acquired. As the facts show, vagrants generally come from an environment where there can be no question of a development of moral qualities. Dr. Bonhoeffer shows, for example, that about 45% of the vagrants examined by him had been brought up in bad home surroundings (alcoholism of the parents, etc.). Then, as we have seen above, the social feelings can be developed only where there is reciprocity. I should like to know whether society really concerns itself with the fate of these unfortunates to such an extent that they in their turn care greatly for the opinion of this same society. Certainly not. They are pariahs, and since they are such the contempt of a hostile world is a matter of indifference.

As we come to the conclusion of our observations upon the etiology of vagrancy and mendicity, we have still but one category to consider, that of those who are indolent by nature. There are individuals in whom assiduous labor of any kind awakens a strong feeling of discomfort. As we have already stated above, in speaking of poverty in general . . . , the cause of this phenomenon is a species of neurasthenia, more especially physical. It is necessary to recognize that, while these individuals are out of harmony with society, they are sick and must be cared for if society is to avoid trouble. Besides, Professor Benedict, who was the first to point out physical neurasthenia, himself recognizes that such sick persons need not become vagrants, if they are brought up in a favorable environment, and that later the struggle for existence will not be painful to them.

To sum up, it is evident that the principal causes of vagrancy and mendicity are lack of work, the want of care for the old, the sick, and the weak, the abandonment of poor children, the low wages and long hours of the workers. The persons who run most danger of being incorporated in the army of vagrants are the weak, whether mentally or physically, but this need not necessarily happen; the "causa causarum" is the environment.

History proves this also. If vagrancy and mendicity sprang from the innate qualities of man, there would always have been vagrants and mendicants, which is not the case. The appearance of these is due to the economic structure of society. It is not possible to discuss this at length and the reader is referred to the work of Florian and Cavaglieri, "I vagabondi." . . . These authors show that the first type of vagrant was the runaway slave, and then the serf who had fled from his lord's domain. In the following periods the penalties with which vagrants were threatened (and they were very severe) were especially designed to force the proletariat to serve the purposes of the possessors of the means of production. In measure as the number of available workers increases and the proletariat submits to the will of the capitalists, this cause becomes less important, and disappears almost completely in our own time. It is rather the contrary that takes place, since the army of vagrants and mendicants is now mainly composed of those who have not been able to find work. Vagabondage and mendicity are at present punishable because of the importunity of the mendicants, the losses experienced by persons living in the country especially, and also because of the danger to society from the fact that the dangerous criminals are partly recruited from this class.

B. Theft and Analogous Crimes

Before examining the motives inducing the commission of theft (the most important crime of this group, the others being mostly modifications of it) we must first stop a moment to ask the question, "Is honesty an innate characteristic or is it acquired?"

In my opinion it is indisputable that honesty is as little innate as any other moral conception. No child can distinguish between mine and thine, it is only little by little that he gains this concept. On the contrary he has the tendency to monopolize everything that he desires (the prehensory instinct, Lafargue names it). It is just this instinct that must be combated to make a child honest. It would, therefore, be more correct to say that dishonesty is innate. Unless one takes account of this fact it is impossible to give the etiology of theft and crimes of the same nature.

The motives for these crimes with which we are now occupied we shall speak of under three heads. The first group includes the crimes committed from *poverty*, the second those that result from cupidity, and in the third group we shall treat of the criminals by profession.

a. Thefts Committed from Poverty

There are some needs which a man must satisfy, without which his existence is impossible. These are fundamental needs, independent of environment. If a man has not sufficient food, if he has not (at least in non-tropical countries) clothing to protect him against cold, if opportunity for rest is lacking, etc., his life is in danger. In our present society there are always a number of persons who are in want of the strict necessaries of life, and who are therefore obliged to steal if they do not wish to succumb to poverty. It is evident that the word "poverty" is not to be taken in the most limited sense, so that one who can still buy a morsel of bread, and yet steals, may still be considered as a thief from poverty.

We must make here one more observation before we enter upon the proofs of this thesis. We have defined crime as an egoistic act. However, the same act may be at once egoistic and altruistic, and this is the case with some crimes committed from poverty, when an individual steals in order not to have those in his charge die of hunger. What conflicts of duty our present society creates!

The proofs that absolute poverty provokes a number of thefts are of three kinds. The first two are based upon the dynamics of criminality.

First. In winter, when poverty is most pressing, the number of thefts, etc., is much greater than in summer.

*   *   *

There is, then, a pretty considerable increase as winter approaches, and a decrease with the summer months. I would call the attention of the reader especially to the fact that it is the crimes of simple theft and the receiving of stolen goods which show this change in the most marked way, while aggravated theft, embezzlement and the professional and habitual receiving of stolen goods show it in less degree. It is the two former crimes which have poverty as their cause, while the three latter are more apt to be committed from cupidity and by professional criminals.

*   *   *

Second. A second proof of the importance of absolute poverty as a cause of crime etc. is furnished by the fact that there is a considerable increase of the crimes in question in times of economic depression (high price of bread, lack of work, etc.).

*   *   *

Few sociological theses, it seems to me, have been proved as conclusively as the one of which we have just been speaking. The important influence of the trend of economic events upon that of economic criminality has been shown for thirteen different countries for different periods of the nineteenth century. Some authors are of the opinion that poverty cannot be the cause of crimes that are committed when economic conditions are most favorable, and when economic crimes have consequently reached their minimum. This assertion still needs fuller proof, as I have already pointed out, since there are still many persons who are in want of the necessaries of life even in times of prosperity.

I must say here a few words in answer to a final objection to the preceding observation; namely, that the increase of theft, etc., in times of economic depression, is, in great part, a consequence, not of absolute poverty, but of the impossibility of satisfying needs that have sprung up in more favorable times; and that the increase will be, therefore, in large measure due to an increase of crimes committed from cupidity, and not from poverty. This may be true in some cases, but not, in my opinion in the great majority of cases, for the following reasons. When the economic situation is favorable, when earnings are more than usual, and when, consequently, wants increase and become more intense, can everyone satisfy the desires awakened in him by the spirit of imitation? Surely not; even at such times of prosperity there are still many individuals with whom desire is awakened but who are not able to satisfy it in a lawful manner. On the other hand, wants in general diminish in times of crisis; cupidity is therefore less excited, and with a limited income men are quite satisfied with having the means of subsistence, when there are so many who lack the very necessaries of life. In my opinion, crimes from cupidity increase rather than diminish in times of prosperity, while in times of depression the opposite takes place. This cannot be proved for each economic crime separately, since criminal statistics do not show whether a crime is committed from poverty or cupidity. However, embezzlement, fraud, and aggravated theft are committed in a greater degree from cupidity than is simple theft (and by professional criminals). Now statistics show that it is chiefly simple theft that follows the course of economic events; the other crimes named doing so much less; the same is true of the changes during the different seasons. Finally, while absolute poverty in countries like Germany has decreased and simple theft also, luxury and cupidity have increased, together with the other crimes named.

The third proof that poverty is a great factor in the etiology of theft is the enormous number of widows and divorced women who participate in these crimes. . . . There is no reason to believe that these women are more covetous than married women or spinsters; but it is certain that their economic situation is often very burdensome.

We shall not employ any further methods to establish our thesis; since for the reasons already stated they would lead to results of no great significance, and it seems that the accuracy of the thesis has been sufficiently shown by the proofs cited.

We have now come to the end of our consideration of the subject of thefts committed from poverty. There are two ways in which it is the cause of theft. On the one hand it incites directly the appropriation of the property of others, and on the other hand it exercises a demoralizing influence.

b. Theft Committed from Cupidity

We have now to deal with crimes of persons who steal neither from absolute poverty, nor by profession. These who are guilty of these crimes earn enough to satisfy their more pressing needs, and they steal only when the occasion presents itself (whence their name of occasional criminals) in order to satisfy their desire for luxury.

The first question, then, which must be answered here is this; how do these needs arise? The answer can be brief; they are aroused by the environment. In a society where some are rich, who have more income than is needed to supply the fundamental necessities, and who create other needs for themselves, in such a society the cupidity of those who have not similar incomes at their disposal will be awakened. The desires which the criminals of whom we are speaking wish to satisfy by their misdeeds are not different from those of the well-to-do. It goes without saying that no one has ever desired any luxury that he has not seen someone else enjoying. It would be a waste of time to discuss this. Every need that is not strictly necessary, is not innate but acquired. If one has much, the other, an imitator, wants the same. There is but one piece of advice to give to those who are not convinced of the simple truth; that they read some ethnological works treating of peoples among whom there are neither rich nor poor. They will then see that cupidity, with us a universal quality, is there unknown.

The division between rich and poor is many centuries old and does not belong to capitalism alone, although under capitalism the distance between the two has greatly increased and is still increasing. The greater this distance is, the more, other things being equal, cupidity increases.

The cupidity of those who can satisfy only the desire for the bare necessities is not awakened in the same measure in each of them. As has already been remarked by Guerry and Quetelet . . . , economic crimes are most numerous in the countries where manufacturing and commerce are most developed, and where the contrasts of fortune are consequently the greatest. It is for this reason that the cities, where the contrasts between poverty and wealth are greatest, give also very high figures for crimes against property. . . .

Those who live in the same country or the same city are not, in spite of that, in the same environment. Every great city has thousands of workers who, because of the character of their labor, have no contact with luxury; others, on the contrary, have the desire for luxury awakened in them by the fact that their work brings them in touch with wealth. Hence it is, for example, that so large a number of economic crimes are committed by workers occupied in commerce . . . , and by servants. There are workmen who have never been accustomed to more than they are able to earn at the time, but there are also those who have known better days and to whom the impossibility of satisfying needs previously acquired is a constant source of suffering.

However, the contrast between rich and poor is not the only cause of the origin of cupidity. We must also sketch, in addition to the above, especially the manner in which commercial capital tries to draw buyers. The times are long gone by when the producer worked principally to order. Modern industry manufactures enormous quantities of goods without the outlet for them being known. The desire to buy must, then, be excited in the public. Beautiful displays, dazzling illuminations, and many other means are used to attain the desired end. The perfection of this system is reached in the great modern retail store, where persons may enter freely, and see and handle everything, where, in short, the public is drawn as a moth to a flame. The result of these tactics is that the cupidity of the crowd is highly excited.

After what has been said it is unnecessary to dwell longer upon the different ways in which cupidity is awakened in our present society. However we must note the following. Almost all the thefts of the class of which we are speaking (those committed by so-called occasional criminals) are thefts of articles of very small value . . . ; the exceptions are the thefts of large sums of money. The authors of these last are in general the employes of banks, etc., persons who, from the nature of their work, have the opportunity to appropriate other people's money. When we investigate the reasons for their committing their misdeeds, we shall see that nine times out of ten (I cannot prove it by figures, but no one will contradict me) the criminal is a speculator who has lost, or perhaps an individual who visits prostitutes, and hence has great need of money.

Cupidity is thus excited by the environment, but not in the same degree in every case, the environment not being the same for all. However, even supposing that the environment were exactly identical for a number of persons, cupidity would not be excited in the same measure in some as in others, since they are not alike, one being born with more intense desires than others (admitting that it is the environment that calls forth the desires). The more intense a man's desires, the more risk he runs, other things being equal, of falling foul of the law. As I have already remarked above, this is important for the person who is seeking the reason why A and not B has stolen, though both live in the same environment; for sociology this fact is only of secondary importance, for it does not ask "*Who* becomes criminal?" but rather "*How* does it happen that there are crimes?"

We have now examined one of the sides of the question; the principal cause of these crimes is the cupidity awakened by the environment. If the environment were different, cupidity would not be aroused and the crimes would not be committed. In my opinion most criminologists do not sufficiently appreciate the importance of this fact. It is very difficult for anyone who lives at ease to form an idea of what is passing in the mind of one who has only the bare necessaries of life and is deprived of every comfort and amusement, while he sees others who have too much, and yet often work less than he does.

Let us now examine the other side of the question. For this purpose let us make use once more of the figure of balances in describing the process that goes on in the brain of the man who hesitates. Upon one of the pans cupidity exercises its force, in different measure according to the person. What are the weights upon the other pan balancing the first? It is the moral forces which must be considered first. I have fully explained above how the economic environment has prevented the social instincts from being developed in man, and how this is especially true for certain classes of persons. It is unnecessary to repeat this here. It will be sufficient to note certain points which have a special importance for the kind of crimes with which we are occupied at the moment.

He who steals, prejudices the interests of another, does him harm, and at the same time injures society, the existence of which would become impossible were theft permitted. In my opinion, the present organization of society, of which the struggle of all against all is the fundamental principle, has reduced this moral factor to very small dimensions. In the economic domain each must be egoistic, for without egoism he would lose in the struggle for existence. In the case of theft and similar crimes, those injured are almost exclusively well-to-do persons, to whom the damage is disagreeable, but who, in general do not suffer much. The thieves, on the other hand, are almost exclusively persons who have to live on very little. How can we expect a poor man to take care not to do a small injury to the rich for fear of causing them a little discomfort, when most rich people are insensible to the suffering which without intermission, overwhelms the poor. The present organization of society is responsible for the fact that a slight sensibility to the misfortune of others offers only a trifling counterpoise to the tendency to realize one's desires in a dishonest manner. The idea that society in itself is injured by theft cannot constitute any considerable counterpoise, since he who violates the eighth commandment cannot feel himself at one with a society which never has helped him when he was in difficulties.

After this general observation let us pass on to particular

remarks that apply to certain classes of persons only. How does it happen that a great proportion of mankind are honest? To this question the answer must be, "because they have been accustomed to it from infancy." The opposite also is true; a great number of thieves are such because any moral education was out of the question in the environment in which they were brought up. They satisfy their "prehensory instinct" without being conscious of any ill-doing. With these the balance inclines to the side of dishonesty, unless a counterpoise of some magnitude is found. Above . . . we have seen that most criminals, especially thieves, come from a totally corrupt environment.

This does not apply to another category of thieves; those who do not proceed from an absolutely corrupt environment—yet whose surroundings are not good and wholesome. Ferriani and Aschaffenburg go so far as to say that almost every child has once stolen something. This may be a little exaggerated but it certainly has truth at the bottom of it. If the child has no one to take the trouble to teach him that he ought not to steal, it is more than likely that he will have to answer for theft later (occasional theft is committed by children and minors especially). It is true that all the children whose education has been defective do not become thieves, nor even the majority of them; there are those for whom a single prohibition will be enough to make them respect the property of others for the rest of their lives. There are others of them, weak characters who, notwithstanding such prohibition, cannot resist when the temptation is strong. If their education had been good, the environment in which they were brought up more favorable, they would not have had to be turned over to justice.

*   *   *

We might close our observations upon theft from cupidity at this point if there were not fear of an objection drawn from what has just been said, namely the following. If the occasional thief has become such, on the one side because of the cupidity awakened in him, and on the other side in consequence of his lack of a good education, and if he differs, not qualitatively, but only quantitatively from the honest man, possessing less strength of character than the average—if all this is true, then the figures for theft should be higher than the statistics show. All of which would go to prove that it is wrong to deny that criminals constitute a biological anomaly.

Here is my reply. First. Moral forces do not constitute the only counterpoise to the tendency toward theft. Since the moral check often lacks efficacy, another has been created which acts in the same way to turn the egoist away from crime, namely the fear inspired by the possibility of punishment. Any one would be credulous indeed to fancy that those who have an opportunity to steal and do not profit by it are deterred by moral forces. Without punishment criminality would be much more extensive than it now is. Where the danger of being found out is not great, the number of transgressions is enormous (think, for example, of the cases of smuggling).

Second. Many persons remain honest, not for moral reasons, but because they lack the courage, cleverness, or other qualities necessary for being otherwise, qualities which in themselves have nothing to do with crime.

Third. Still others remain honest for reasons based upon mature reflection. They find that it is too dangerous to commit an offense, but do not hesitate in the presence of acts *essentially* criminal, although they do not fall under the ban of the law. No one is ignorant of this, and only certain anthropologists who examine no one but prisoners, have lost sight of it.

Those who compose the criminal world are by nature very diverse. Some are the most dangerous individuals that it is possible to imagine, others are rather weak than wicked. Among these last are ranged the occasional criminals, who, taken together, form a danger to society, but taken singly are not dangerous men in the strict sense. Leuss, who learned to know prisoners, not as judge, or as medical expert, but as a prisoner himself, says: "The great mass of prisoners are more good-natured than the average man; the good-nature of thieves corresponds with their weakness of will, that invincible obstacle to their maintaining themselves in the world of industry. Stress must constantly be laid upon the fact that these weak-willed, good-natured persons are the ones who swell the number of crimes."

When we place beside the occasional thieves, those who never steal but commit all sorts of reprehensible (though not illegal) acts, the comparison is not to the advantage of the latter. Their trickery, their pitiless egoism, often make them more dangerous to society than the others; which should be a reason for criminal anthropology not to build a system based solely upon investigations of prisoners.

Fourth. Finally, many more crimes are committed than are mentioned by criminal statistics. Although I have already spoken of this . . . , I must return to it. In the first place, most criminal statistics give the figures only for those convicted. Those acquitted have no place, although, with few exceptions, a crime has nevertheless been committed. We know that the number of acquittals is very considerable. In Germany, there were 15 to 20 acquittals to 100 cases tried (1882–1896); in Italy the number of acquittals ran as high as 51.37% (1890–1895).

In the second place, in many cases the prosecution is postponed for different reasons, with the result that there is neither an acquittal nor a condemnation. Then a great many cases never come to trial because justice cannot discover the authors of the crimes. In Germany, for example, of all the cases on the dockets in the criminal courts between 1881 and 1891, only 43 to 45% actually came before the judges. During the period between 1886 and 1890, the examining judges dismissed on an average 8900 cases, either because the author of the crime was unknown, or because the proof was insufficient. During the same period and for the same reasons, 98,741 cases on the average were not prosecuted by the authorities. The authors of about 25% of the crimes committed in Italy remained unknown (1887–1894).

These two reasons by themselves show that the number of crimes is much greater than the statistics would generally lead one to suppose, even if one takes account of the fact that some of the complaints made to the prosecutors are false.

In the third place, we have been speaking so far of the cases that come to the notice of the officers, while in a great number of cases no complaint is made, especially in the matter of petty theft, either because the person injured wishes to avoid the annoyance of having to appear in the police court as witness, or because he wishes to spare the delinquent.

In the fourth place, a great many small thefts remain unknown even to the person injured, since he does not notice the loss that he has suffered.

All this goes to show that crime, taken in the strict sense, and especially theft, is much more extensive than one would expect at first, and the objection that might have been made to my thesis is hence without weight. It is evident that the number of criminals unpunished cannot be fixed with certainty. Dr. Puibaraud places it at 50%; while Tarde believes that it is greater; Yvernès, the well-known French statistician, says that 90% of the professional thieves remain unknown, and Dr. Thomsen, from whom I take this last fact, says that this applies to other categories of criminals also. However this may be, the number in any case is very considerable.

To sum up. I believe I have shown that the fundamental causes of theft and similar crimes committed from cupidity are, on the one hand, the cupidity aroused by the environment and, on the other, neglected childhood among the poor. It is especially those weak in character who run the greatest risk of becoming guilty of these crimes.

c. *Crimes Committed by Professional Criminals*

In considering all the kinds of theft and analogous crimes, we note that the thefts committed by professional criminals represent only a minority. But as soon as we limit our consideration to the more serious forms of theft, such as burglary and similar crimes, we shall discover that they are committed almost exclusively by individuals whose principal or subsidiary occupation is theft, and who, in general, do not consider it shameful, and do not feel the slightest repentance.

The question arises, how it is possible for anyone to embrace so abject a profession, and thus become so harmful a parasite. There are authors who would have us believe that there are persons who have chosen crime from pleasure in it. As Leuss observes in his work, "Aus dem Zuchthause," this opinion is so absurd that it would be a waste of time to consider it. No one of sound mind could possibly prefer so abominable a profession, and one so full of risks from the point of view of simple calculation. There must be other reasons for the existence of such persons. If we wish to examine these causes we must divide professional criminals into separate groups.

The first category is composed of children. Sad as this is it is none the less true. It is plain that not a single child follows the profession of thief from pleasure, for a child prefers not to work at all. These children, then, are taught to steal by their parents. If they are not very numerous, in the great cities there are always some cases of this kind.

* * *

Now, as for the others, those who have not been brought up for a life of crime, yet practice it as their profession—how can we explain their manner of life? The answer to this question can be found only in the works of those who have familiarized themselves with the life of criminals, and who have lived in their midst in order to know them (like Flynt, for example), or who are in a position, because of their profession, to study them in detail, and become their confidants (like the well-known almoners of the Grande-Roquette: Crozes, Moreau, and Faure).

Except for a few subsidiary circumstances the life of the professional criminal may be summed up as follows. With very rare exceptions he springs from a corrupt environment, perhaps having lost his parents while still very young, or having even been abandoned by them. Being misled by bad company, he commits an "occasional" theft while still a child, for which he must pay the penalty of an imprisonment; he may, at times owe his entrance into prison to a non-economic misdeed. This, however, is a very rare exception. As we have remarked above, prison never improves him, and generally makes him worse. If he is in contact with the other prisoners, among whom there are naturally a number of out and out criminals, he hears the recital of their adventurous life, learns their tricks and all that he still needs to know to be thoroughly informed as to "the profession." Nor will the separate cell be any more profitable to him, brutalized as he already is by his earlier environment. Then after a certain time he is set at liberty and returned to society. The partisans of free will say that he has expiated his fault and can now commence a new life.

That is easy to say, and certainly justice will not concern itself with him any further until he commits a new offense. But this is not the same as saying that society pardons him and aids him, in order that he may remain in the right path. On the contrary, forgetting that we must forgive those who have trespassed against us, society makes life hard for him. It is almost impossible for him to find work; the fact that he has been in prison is enough to insure his being refused everywhere. Why should anyone hire an old prisoner when there are so many others who have never got into the courts? And then most prisoners have never learned a trade, and this is one reason more why they cannot easily find employment. The liberated convict becomes a nomad, begins by losing all contact with the normal world (supposing he ever had any) and feels himself a social pariah. On the other hand he has relations more and more frequent with the "under world," with those who recognize no duty toward a society which is not interested in their fate. His moral sense comes to be more and more blunted until he becomes a criminal by profession, having a feeling neither of shame nor of repentance.

The ignorant public, who know nothing about the professional criminal except when he appears before the tribunal, is astonished to find that there are persons so abject. This astonishment is like that of some one who has never seen a house built, and cannot imagine how such a colossus can be put up. But he who has seen how the house has been erected by adding one small brick to another no longer feels any astonishment. It is the same with the professional criminal; he who has followed the story of the criminal's life recognized with Dr. Havelock Ellis, that his crime is but the last link of a solidly forged chain.

Generally the professional criminal does not give the least sign of repentance. He does as much injury to society as he can, without having any shame about it. Yet he is not entirely deprived of moral sense, only it extends merely to those who are really his fellows. All the tales of the world of professional criminals which depict them as void of all sense of duty toward their fellows, proceed rather from the imagination of the authors than from facts really observed. The only competent authors are those who have been able to study the criminal *in his own environment,* and not in prison, where his true character makes itself known as little as that of an animal in a cage. Hear the opinion of Flynt, for example. "It is often said that his (the professional criminal's) lack of remorse for his crimes proves him to be morally incompetent; but this opinion is formed on insufficient knowledge of his life. He has two systems of morality: one for his business and the other for the hang-out."

*   *   *

It is plain that the manner in which criminals act toward a society that is hostile to them will not fail to influence the relations they have with their fellows, just as war for those who take part in it cannot leave their moral sense as regards their compatriots unharmed. However, nothing permits us to put the actions of these persons among themselves in the same rank as those towards society. In my opinion this fact has great significance for the moralist and the criminologist; it is one of the forms of the dualism of ethics. It is of very high importance for the criminologist, for it shows that we are upon the wrong track, since it is precisely the more serious forms of crime that the present methods of repression favor.

In imprisoning young people who have committed merely misdemeanors of minor importance, and who have not yet lost all touch with normal society, and putting them in contact with inveterate criminals, or perhaps putting them into a cage like beasts, without striving to enlighten their darkened minds or teach them morality, and without making them capable of sustaining the struggle for existence by teaching them a trade, we are bringing up professional criminals. Punishment, as a means of intimidation, misses its aim in great part, for the professional criminals are recruited among individuals who are not easily intimidated.

We have now come to the question why a certain number only of those whose childhood has been neglected and who have committed a light offense, become professional criminals. In the first place there are those whom chance favors, since they are assisted, it may be by their families, it may be by some philanthropist, and so return to the right path. There are those also who have the advantage of being able to find work, since no one knows that they have been in prison.

Others have less chance; no one aids them, there is no work for them; all, however, do not become professional thieves. Those who become such are the more intelligent, energetic, ambitious, and courageous of these outcasts; the others become vagrants and mendicants. Here is the opinion of Flynt upon the criminal by profession, an opinion which agrees with that of other competent authors. "I must say . . . that those criminals who are known to me are not, as is also popularly supposed, the scum of their environment. On the contrary, they are above their environment, and are often gifted with talents which would enable them to do well in any class, could they only be brought to realize its responsibilities and to take advantage of its opportunities. The notion that the criminal is the lowest type of his class arises from a false conception of that class and of the people who compose it. . . .

"In this same class, however, there are some who are born with ambitions, and who have energy enough to try to fulfil them. These break away from class conditions; but unfortunately, the ladder of respectable business has no foothold in their environment. . . .

"Not all of these ambitious ones are endowed with an equal amount of energy. Some are capable only of tramp life, which, despite its many trials and vicissitudes, is more attractive than the life they seek to escape. Those with greater energy go into crime proper; and they may be called, mentally as well as physically, the aristocracy of their class. This is my analysis of the majority of the criminal men and women I have encountered in the open, and I believe it will hold good throughout their entire class."

There are readers, perhaps, who will find that these qualities of the professional criminal give the lie to the environment hypothesis, since individual factors are recognized in a certain way. For myself I do not find it so. The qualities mentioned have nothing to do with crime as such; they can be utilized to the profit as well as to the detriment of society; it will depend upon the environment in which the individual endowed with them has been raised what direction he will take. It would not be difficult to name a number of historic celebrities (Napoleon, for example) who, if they had been born in the lower stratum of a great city, in place of in a favorable environment, would have had only the sad celebrity of criminals exceptionally endowed.

The psychology of this kind of criminals is not yet complete however. Besides intelligence, energy, and courage we find cupidity as their great characteristic. They see others who can enjoy themselves without working hard, and it is their ambition to do the same, cost what it may. Since fate has made it impossible for them to attain it honestly they risk another method. This type of criminal is well delineated in the remark made by the notorious Lemaire, when he said to the president of the court: "If I were a property owner, I should not be here."

To have invested funds, to spend plenty of money, not to have to work much, this is their ideal; to share the lot of the working-man, who, notwithstanding his long and hard labor, never succeeds in procuring for himself the pleasures of the rich, makes life insipid in their eyes. M. Gisquet, former prefect of police, gives in his memoirs the following declaration made by Leblanc, the notorious professional criminal. "If I were not a thief by vocation I should become one by calculation; it is the best profession. I have computed the good and bad chances of all the others, and I am convinced by the comparisons that there is none more favorable or more independent than that of thief, nor one that does not offer at least an equal amount of danger.

"What should I have become in the society of honest men? A natural child, with no one to protect me or to recommend me, I could only choose a disagreeable trade, become a delivery-boy in a store, or at most reach the miserable place of shipping clerk in a warehouse; and there, a supernumerary for many years, I should have died of hunger before I reached a salary of six hundred francs. As a workman in any class whatever you exhaust yourself quickly through the fatigues of your labor, to earn a miserable wage, and to live from day to day; then when accident, sickness, or old age come you must go beg or die in the poorhouse. . . .

"In our condition we depend only on ourselves; and if we acquire skill and experience at least they profit ourselves alone. I know very well that we have risks to run, that the police and the courts are at hand, that the prison is not very far distant; but out of eight thousand thieves in Paris, you never have more than seven or eight hundred in jail; that is not a tenth of the whole. We enjoy, then, on the average, nine years of liberty to one in prison. Well, where is the worker who has not a dead season? Besides, what does he do when he is without work? He carries his possessions to the Mont-de-Piété; while we others, if we are free, lack for nothing; our existence is a continual round of feasting and pleasure."

This is the type of the perfect egoist. In ranking men according to their social sentiments, such an individual would be put at the very lowest point in the scale. And then he has grown up under unfavorable circumstances (illegitimate birth, etc.). The innate egoism of this individual may perhaps be modified by the individual factor. But this in no way diminishes the truth of the environment hypothesis, for we are treating for the moment the question why this *particular individual* has become a criminal, and not that of the cause of the existence of professional criminals. And these two questions are far from being identical. The existence of individual differences is the reason why one *runs more danger* of becoming a professional criminal than another; but it is the environment which brings it about that the predisposed individual *actually* becomes such. The falsity of the environment hypothesis would be demonstrated if such individuals could be proved to become criminals *under all circumstances*. This is of course not the case. When individuals like these are not brought up in an atmosphere of poverty, they no longer see on the one side persons who enjoy everything while doing nothing, and on the other side those who, while toiling hard, live in poverty,—they will not become examples of altruism indeed, but they will not become guilty of crime. They may even become very useful members of society, since they are generally more largely endowed with intelligence, energy, and courage than the average man. Rightly exercised, these qualities are very useful; but badly directed they are very harmful to society.

So far we have been treating of the etiology of theft and analogous crimes; we shall conclude this section with some observations upon the causes that have led to the designating of these acts as crime.

Theft is a crime only because it is very harmful to society. If in the majority of cases the individual does not take account of this, the assertion is nevertheless true. Everything that is harmful to society the individual considers as immoral. (*Why* this is so is a psychological question, with which we are not concerned here.) If we picture to ourselves present-day society, based as it is upon exchange, without the strict prohibition of theft, we shall see that it could not possibly exist. Life would be especially impossible in a society where the division of labor has attained a high degree of development, if it were permissible to take anything without giving an equivalent.

Since the human race has existed there has been private property, however trifling and unimportant it may have been. It is therefore very unlikely that theft has ever been permitted (it is impossible to produce proofs in support of this), since it is difficult to imagine that anyone would consent to see himself stripped of things destined for his own use, to which, further he was more or less attached. But there is a great difference between a prohibited act and a crime. It is proved that among primitive peoples theft is not reckoned among the crimes. Hear the opinion of one of the greatest specialists in this field, Dr. Post. "We find here and there a phenomenon very surprising from our modern point of view, namely that theft is not universally regarded as a misdemeanor, but the thief rather respected for his cleverness. The maximum obligation that a theft lays upon the thief is simple restitution of the stolen property. The consequence of theft is thus simply the duty of restitution under the civil law. . . . Theft lies entirely outside of the province of criminal law."

It is not difficult to explain the cause of this. Let the reader picture to himself the primitive forms of society, so different from those we have at present; contrasts of possessions were unknown, and the needs of men consequently less numerous; men produced only for their own consumption and not for exchange. If by chance more was produced than was needed, the surplus was given to others, for it was impossible to exchange it, or to preserve it for any great length of time, the necessary technique for this not having yet been acquired. "The law of hospitality" was universal and enjoined men to provide those in need with whatever they lacked. It is quite comprehensible that at such a stage of development theft should not be in evidence, for the motives which drive men to it would be lacking. On the one hand cupidity was not awakened, and theft did not result from absolute poverty, since if there was poverty the whole group suffered together. On the other hand the social instincts, being highly developed by the environment, constituted a restraint that would prevent the execution of a theft if the thought of it should occur. But even supposing that in such a society a theft, for no matter what cause, should nevertheless be committed, it would be little thought of, and certainly the thief would not be severely punished, for his act would not be very harmful to society.

As the social structure changed the ideas about theft changed equally; with the origin of the system of exchange and of the contrasts of property, came powerful motives for theft, and at the same time the social instincts grew weaker. Thus theft came to be considered a more serious matter than before, and the graded system of punishments for it, beginning with a fine, ended in capital punishment. It is not our task to investigate the reason why the punishment for theft has not always been the same during the whole civilized period; it is enough for us to establish the fact that the act has always been considered as a grave offense, the perpetrator of which incurred severe penalties.

C. Robbery and Analogous Crimes

As the figures reproduced above . . . have shown, the crimes with which we have now to concern ourselves are relatively rare. It is unnecessary to say that this has not always been so, but that there have been great changes in this regard. At one time robbery and similar acts of violence were the ordinary forms of professional crime. Happily for peaceable folk this is no longer the case; these crimes have been in large measure replaced by others less serious; like theft and fraud. All modern states have not reached the same stage of development, nor all parts of the same state. There are those of them that, more than others, recall the past to us. So is it in regard to their criminality. While robbery may be said to have disappeared from the states of northern Europe, it is still very common in a country like Italy, and is met much less frequently in the modernized provinces of northern Italy than in the backward southern provinces, as the following figures show.

❖   ❖   ❖

According to the figures given by Dr. Bosco, in the United States, also, the most backward states give the highest figures for homicide.

The poorer classes have more resemblance to the people of a bygone day than have the well-to-do; it appears from the statistics . . . that economic criminality takes a more violent form among the former than among the latter.

An investigation into the causes of this change in the form of economic criminality will indicate also the principal causes of the persistent existence of this kind of crime, however it may have decreased in modern times. In my opinion these causes are as follows:

First. The opportunity for committing them presented itself more often formerly, since the means of communication were very primitive, travelers had to traverse uninhabited countries, etc., and in addition the states were not so well organized as at present, and had not the means of suppressing bands of brigands vigorously.

Second. While the opportunity to commit violent economic crimes successfully was diminishing, there was a constantly increasing opportunity to commit other economic crimes, such as theft, embezzlement, and fraud. The accumulation of great wealth in the cities, the development of credit, in short, the enormous extension of capitalism, has multiplied the opportunity for economic crimes without violence.

Third. One of the consequences of the development of society has been the gradual diminution of the importance of the rôle played by violence, and, since criminality presents itself always and everywhere under the same forms as the normal life, violent economic criminality has also commenced to form a smaller and smaller part in the totality of economic crimes. The assertion that violence has lost the importance of its rôle upon the human stage might surprise one, and appear ironical in times like ours when war is the chronic condition, when the military preparations of all the states have reached a degree hitherto unknown. Violence, however, has decreased in so far as it is exercised by the individual as such. The greater becomes the centralization of the state, the more it claims for itself the exclusive right to use violence in the cases where it judges it necessary, and the more it prohibits individual acts of violence.

It is not the development of the state that is alone to be considered in this regard; the economic system enters in also. Under capitalism violence is of no use; he who is master of the means of production attains his end, *i.e.*, makes a profit, without the use of violence. Where it is necessary, however, modern man does not recoil from it, as the wars of expansion prove.

Fourth. Civilization (in the proper sense of the word) has become more general. Formerly the privilege of a few only, it now extends to a greater number. The great mass are still deprived of it, but primary instruction contributes to its development.

When we consider the gradual diminution in the number of economic crimes committed with violence, it clearly appears how false is the notion that anyone committing such a crime is for that reason a *biologically* abnormal being. Will anyone claim that the number of biologically abnormal persons has constantly diminished? The contrary is much more likely.

We need not concern ourselves with the details of this question, since it has already been thoroughly treated by Professor Manouvrier. . . . He who uses violence to attain an economic end may perhaps, physiologically considered, be a perfectly normal man. How many children are there who do not use force to take a toy from a weaker child? Must we class them as abnormal on that account? And are those who voluntarily take part in a war abnormal? Certainly there is a great difference between those who take part in a war, and those who, for economic reasons, commit a crime, but this difference is of a *social* nature. Our ideas of war and homicide are not the same, but the act of killing one's neighbor remains identical. If homicide were the evident proof of biological abnormality the soldier also would be abnormal.

Scientific questions can be solved by reason alone, and not by sentiment. We who experience a profound repulsion at the thought of a murderer, hold him for a being apart, since we feel ourselves so remote from him. Scientific research tells us that this feeling is not innate but acquired, for we detest such acts because the environment in which we live has accustomed us to hate them. If our environment were different, our feelings would likewise be different. Besides, war proves that these feelings are not innate, by hardening the mildest persons in a very brief time.

With time the number of persons who have a horror of violence has increased. Does this prove that men have become better, or simply that they feel a repugnance to the act only and not to its effect? J. J. Rousseau once said: "If, in order to fall heir to the property of a rich mandarin living at the farthest confines of China, whom one had never seen or heard spoken of, it were enough to push a button to make him die, which of us would not push that button?"

It is certain that beside a great number of persons who would not wish to charge their consciences with such a crime, there would also be plenty who would commit it, and their number would be great enough to make the order of mandarins pass into legendary history. There is no reason to suppose that there are fewer persons in our day who would commit such acts, than formerly; if men are no longer as violent as they once were, they do not recoil any more than formerly when it is a question of suppressing, through the agency of a third party, those who oppose them; as witness the wars of expansion.

As the motives of these crimes are the same as those of economic crimes without violence, we shall treat first those that are caused by poverty; secondly, those that are committed from cupidity; and thirdly, those that are the work of professional criminals.

Statistics show that a part of the economic crimes of violence are committed from poverty, for their movement is influenced by the fluctuations of economic conditions.

❊   ❊   ❊

Although these data are less numerous than we might desire, they show sufficiently that, in part, violent economic crimes are committed because of poverty.

Above I have shown how it happens that only some of those who live in absolute poverty commit crime. We have only, then, to ask ourselves why one commits a crime with violence and the other without violence. The causes are of different kinds. Oftenest it is chance, *i.e.* opportunity, that is the cause. No one uses violence if it is not necessary, and since the opportunity of committing a successful theft is much greater than that of committing an economic crime with violence, it is the first that is most often practiced. Those who, when driven by abject poverty, commit an economic crime with violence, when the opportunity presents itself, are persons who lack neither the force nor the courage necessary, and in whom the environment in which they live has not inspired a great aversion to violence. Further, absolute poverty is so powerful a factor that it often neutralizes the important influences of education and environment.

From cupidity. The class of criminals who use violence or commit a homicide from cupidity is very small. They furnish only a minor part of violent economic crimes, the total number of which is not itself very great. To show how far the influence of economic environment goes I will cite some striking cases taken at random.

First. In 1892 a certain Scheffer was convicted at Linz (Austria) of attempted murder. His crime was the following. He and his wife could earn their living only by working hard. Chance brought a change. One of their relatives, a young girl who had lost her father and mother a short time before, came to live with them. The girl being very rich, the condition of the Scheffers was entirely changed; from then on they could live in abundance. Once habituated to this wealth they were filled with the fear that their relative would marry and the money pass to someone else. Little by little the idea came to them of persuading the girl to make a will in their favor, and then killing her, an idea which they rejected at first, but which nevertheless became stronger and stronger. From unforeseen circumstances the crime was never consummated, but stopped in the attempt.

Second. In a little village upon the frontier of Austria and Bavaria there was committed in 1893 a murder under the following circumstances. One evening, while returning by himself along a lonely road, a rich peasant who was in the habit of carrying a considerable sum of money with him, was killed and robbed. It was proved that his servant was the author of the crime. This man was a natural child, very poor, and had had to work very hard all his life. Seeing his strength going he was in great fear of being no longer able to earn a living. His sole enjoyment in his monotonous and toilsome life was getting drunk on Sundays. Like most of the inhabitants of his commune he was an ardent poacher.

Third. In 1892 the wife of an employe of the post office was assassinated in her dwelling in Berlin, and all her money stolen. The criminals were two young workmen of 17 and 18 years of age, one of whom knew by chance that the woman had savings.

These three cases, types of hundreds of others, have in common the opportunity which had excited, in an unusual degree, the cupidity of the criminals, and the fact that these were very poor. Whatever other causes may have entered in, it is certain that without the great difference of fortune between the authors of the crimes and their victims, the crimes would never have been committed.

Finally, we come to the influence of the environment upon the authors of the crimes. As we have seen, the conditions under which criminals are brought up are in general very unfavorable, and this is especially the case with dangerous criminals. Consider, for example, the second case (we know nothing of the environment of the criminals in the first). What a life this murderer had behind him. The influences which give most men their aversion to violence were entirely lacking. On the contrary his environment had brutalized him. A natural child, he had been brought up in very poor circumstances, and was stupefied by long and toilsome work, with a weekly intoxication as his sole relaxation. No one would assert that this same individual would have become an assassin if he had lived under totally different conditions.

Or look at the third case. One of the guilty parties had been brought up under unfavorable conditions (of the education of the other we know nothing), both were forced, quite young, to earn their living and had been thrown with bad companions, and one of them had already been sentenced to imprisonment.

It is a mistake to believe that such a case is the exception instead of being the general rule. He who takes the trouble to read the biographies of these criminals knows that they have always been brought up in an unfavorable environment, that they have suffered imprisonment at an early age, and have fallen lower and lower.

* * *

We have still to fix our attention upon one side of the environment in which the authors of the crimes with which we are concerned at the moment, have lived. They come generally from an environment where;

First, education often consists simply in the administration of a sound beating to the child, a fact which habituates him to the idea that violence is an ordinary act, especially as he sees the members of the family often strike one another;

Second, the men ordinarily carry a knife, and do not hesitate to threaten with it, or even to use it in case of a dispute. It is evident that the influence of this upon character is great at the impressionable age of childhood. The tendency toward violence, combated among children of the well-to-do classes, is, on the contrary, often strengthened among the children of the poor. If later chance places in their way an opportunity to profit by violence they recoil from it less than others.

The authors of violent economic crimes spring nearly always from the lower classes of the population; the exceptions are few in number. We will take up one of these exceptions which has attained considerable notoriety, an evident proof of the rarity of these cases.

In 1878 an old woman was murdered in Paris and all her papers of value were stolen. It was proved that Barré, a business agent, and Lebiez, a medical student, both of whom had passed their youth in a favorable environment, were the guilty persons. This is one of those very rare cases where objection can be made to the environment hypothesis with a semblance of truth, but a closer examination shows that environment nevertheless played its part in this frightful tragedy. The two criminals, sprung from fairly well-to-do provincial families, having gone to Paris, had been living in straitened circumstances. At the time of their deciding to commit the crime their pecuniary condition was very bad. In the second place, both had constant recourse to prostitutes; and in the third place both were ardent speculators. Because of his business Barré was in contact with those who gambled at the bourse, and seeing men enrich themselves without work he entered feverishly into speculation. He lost, drew his father into a new deal, and was still unfortunate. In order to go on and retrieve his losses he used money entrusted to him (his first crime), but still lost. Going from one malversation to another he finally, in order to extricate himself, had recourse to the crime narrated above. His accomplice was found in nearly the same situation.

The effect of environment is to be discerned, then, as easily in this case as in those that have been referred to before. Limiting ourselves to the principal influence alone, we see that if these individuals had not been in contact with the world of speculation, their cupidity would not have been excited to such a point that they were induced to commit crime. Here the rôle played by chance in such cases clearly appears; if they had been fortunate in their speculations they would never have become criminals.

As with all crimes, the question presents itself as to how far individual factors were active, in other words, do the individuals who are guilty of such crimes differ from other men? Certainly, and that to a considerable extent. But in granting this we do not, however, recognize a *qualitative* difference between them and other men such as would make them *biologically abnormal*. The motives which have induced these persons to commit crime, are present, though only in small measure, in everyone. Those who commit these crimes have by nature very intense material needs. . . . As regards their social sentiments . . . , their repugnance to violence is very small. Further, they have the necessary courage and strength. If we consider how little chance there is of finding all this united in one individual, it will become clear that few individuals are predisposed to these crimes, and when they are committed the criminal is found in a special environment. In my opinion there can be no question of individual factors, then; it is the environment that decides here. There will be persons always and everywhere who run more danger than others of committing such a crime; but it is the environment which will decide whether they will commit it or not.

Professional criminals. The great majority of violent economic crimes are committed by professional criminals. When an individual has fallen, from whatever reason, into the world of professional crime, sooner or later comes the time when he must use violence if he wishes to attain his end. Joly has very well said in his social study, "Le crime": "The man who has formed the habit of breaking into houses and bursting open safes, is forcibly drawn sooner or later to rid himself of witnesses who surprise him at his work, or of a victim who might perhaps recognize him." It cannot be asserted of these individuals any more than of others, that they are born with a special tendency toward assassination, a tendency to be explained by atavism, or something approaching it. They have been living in an environment in which such acts are considered as a necessary evil inherent in their trade. Driven by the tendency to imitate, they do as others do. Certainly there are those of them who do not commit these crimes, but that proves nothing, for it may be that chance has favored them and they have never been under the necessity of using violence, or they have less courage and force than the average man, or, it may be, have an exceptional innate aversion to violence.

As Professor Manouvrier remarks, the case would be entirely different if such criminals killed without plausible motives, if they committed murder without anything but the act in view. The facts show that this is not so. Note the opinion of Flynt. "The taking of life is . . . [a] deed that he [the professional criminal] regrets more than he has been given credit for. One thinks of the criminal as the man who has no respect for life, as one who takes it without any twitchings of conscience; but this is not the general rule. The business criminal never takes a life, if he can help it."

We need not treat here of the causes which have led to the designating of these acts as crimes; they are the same as those given above in connection with economic crimes without violence. The harm done by these crimes is naturally greater than in the case of crimes without violence, since they put life as well as property in danger. It is interesting to note here, once more, the dualism of ethics; many primitive peoples consider these acts as crimes when they are committed within the same group, but very honorable when once the act passes beyond the limits of the group. Further, with modern peoples this difference still persists: colonial wars often resemble a colossal robbery.

D. Fraudulent Bankruptcy, Adulteration of Food, and Analogous Crimes

We reach now the last group of economic crimes, those which are committed wholly, or in great part, by the bourgeoisie. The motives of these crimes are not all the same; here too it is necessary to make distinctions. The categories into which we must distribute the motives leading to these crimes are analogous to those which lead to theft etc., poverty and cupidity. And as in the case of theft it is necessary to add a third category, that of the great criminals, who can be compared with criminals by profession.

The first category may be compared with that of theft committed from poverty; those who fall in this class are persons who, for one reason or another, have seen their business decline, and not knowing any other way to escape from their difficulties, hope to retrieve their losses and save themselves by committing a misdeed. I take from Moreau's "Le Monde des Prisons" a typical case. After having described how a certain R. had succeeded in setting himself up in business and had been successful, the author speaks as follows. "Unhappily the panic caught him among the first. His business became worse and worse. In a few months he lost several thousand francs. Two of his traveling salesmen ran off with their foods. Orders ceased coming in. It was failure, dishonor. He fought, but was wrecked. . . ." Finally, in order to escape ruin he committed a breach of trust; he was discovered and convicted.

We cannot say that it is absolute poverty that drives these persons to commit a crime, for generally they have enough left to keep them from dying of hunger. And if not, they are generally members of families who are in a position to keep them from the worst poverty. Further they can try to provide for their wants by paid labor. Nevertheless these cases are somewhat analogous to those of absolute poverty. Picture to yourself the state of mind of one who has led a more or less comfortable life, who has been independent, and enjoyed the esteem granted to a man who is well-to-do, and who sees that the time is approaching when all this will come to an end, and that there remains nothing for him to do but accept some minor poorly paid employment, and lead henceforth an existence that cannot satisfy him in any way. Imagine also that chance throws in his way an opportunity to commit a crime with good hope of success. It must be granted that we find here very powerful determinants to crime.

This cause of crimes of this class is of an entirely social nature. Under another mode of production, for example, under that of village communities, the idea of committing such crimes could not arise. For this reason we cannot say that social causes have often nothing to do with the matter, but that it is the man's own fault if his business goes to pieces. This is certainly true at times; but it is the present organization of society which makes it possible for a man to be in charge of an enterprise which he is not fitted to conduct, while another who is fitted for it cannot find employment for his talents. It is only in a society where complete anarchy reigns in the economic life, that it is possible for a man to think he is capable of directing a business merely because he happens to have capital.

Let us now examine the other side of the question. What are

the forces capable of preventing these projects from being realized? First let us ask, what is the environment in which many
of these individuals who are guilty of such crimes are brought
up? Certainly they have learned that one must be honest, that
it is wrong to pick pockets, etc., and they will not fail in this
regard. But they have learned also that the principal end in life
is to grow rich, to succeed. Too often this is contrary to the
principle of probity. "Be honest, be honest, if possible, but . . .
make money!" This is the principal rule imprinted upon the
minds of the children in certain bourgeois environments. It is
an honesty of a special kind that is inculcated, not a moral honesty, but an honesty for the sake of one's own interests. "Honesty
is the best policy," says the quasi-moral precept. Those whose
probity has this for a basis have only a weak check to prevent
them from becoming criminal, when the thought of the wrong
act arises within them. They remain honest so long as it is to their
advantage, but woe to society when this is no longer the case.

But further, the environment in which these persons have
lived after their youth has not contributed to reinforce the social
sentiments, and consequently those that are working in an anti-
criminal direction. "Every man for himself" is the principle of
success in such an environment. It is evident that the social
sentiments must be strongly opposed in their development if the
maxim just given is that which dominates. To act morally implies
sacrificing one's own advantage for the sake of the general good.
He who is compelled always to have his own interests at heart
can give very little thought to the interests of others.

As in the case of all crimes, it is necessary with regard to these
also to put the question, are the individuals who are guilty of
them, as regards their innate qualities, like those who have lived
and still live under the same conditions? And as is the case with
all crimes, the answer here must be in the negative. Those who
are guilty of these crimes are, in general, those who are below
the average in the strength of their moral qualities. They are
rather weak than bad; they are conscious of the harm that they

do to others and are ashamed of it, but they are too weak to resist the pressure of circumstances. As always it is the environment that is the cause of the crimes' taking place; it is the individual differences which explain in part *who* is the one to commit them. Adapting the well-known sentence of Quetelet we may say, "it is society that prepares the crimes, it is the men of inferior moral caliber who execute them." If the environment were entirely different the men of inferior moral caliber would not be guilty of crime.

It may be observed, perhaps, that if it is true that a special predisposition on the part of the individual is unnecessary for the explanation of these crimes, they ought to be more numerous than they are. This is true enough, but it does not refute the opinion which has been expressed. For, first, as is the case with all the others, these crimes are more numerous than the criminal statistics show; second, there are reasons why some men do not commit crime, although all circumstances lead to it, and their moral condition does not prevent. For example, there are those who, as a consequence of the struggle for existence, have lost all energy and all courage, and give up the fight, even the fight with dishonest weapons; others, prudent by nature, take into consideration the fact that, bad as their situation may be, it would be worse if the crime were discovered, etc.

Statistics prove that it is really the decline of business that is the cause of a great number of bourgeois crimes.

* * *

These statistics, to be sure, are not numerous, since the number of crimes committed by the bourgeoisie is small, and the other economic crimes, like theft, for example, are much more important, and hence draw the attention of statisticians more.

We come now to the second category; bourgeois economic crimes from cupidity (as is always the case, the line of demarcation between this group and the preceding one is not distinctly traced, there being many gradations between the two). They are committed, not, as in the first category, by those whose business is declining, but by those whose affairs are more or less flourishing. The only motive, then, is cupidity; what they get by honest business is not enough for them, they wish to become richer. After what has been already said about cupidity it is unnecessary to go into detail here. It has been shown that it is only under certain special circumstances that this desire for wealth arises, and that it is unknown under others. It will be necessary only to point out the fact that although cupidity is a strong motive with all classes of our present society, it is especially so among the bourgeoisie, as a consequence of their position in the economic life. This, then, is the first and most important cause of these crimes, a cause which is not individual, but entirely of a social nature.

In the second place, the opportunity to commit these offenses undetected is enormous (I refer especially to the adulteration of food). In general the consumer cannot judge whether the merchandise is pure or not, and in most cases there is no inspection by experts, or else it is worthless, since the experts are named by the producers themselves.

In the third place, we have to ask ourselves, in what way does the environment in which these persons live exercise an influence upon their social sentiments? We have already called attention to this point some pages above, and can be brief therefore. This environment tends to weaken the social sentiments which might act as a check upon very egoistic acts.

Considered from the point of view of the consumer, the adulteration of food products is a grave crime, for it injures the health and may even endanger the life. But what *moral* impropriety will be seen in it by a producer who derives great profits from the exploitation of children, or who, by a corner in grain, causes a great increase in the price of bread? Is there, sociologically speaking, a difference between these two groups of acts? Certainly not; the one is as harmful as the other, nay, the last two probably more harmful than the first.

This kind of crime must be the despair of those who seek for some biological anomaly of the criminal as the primary cause of crime, for here the anomaly forms almost the rule. Dr. Puibaraud, in his "Malfaiteurs de profession," rightly says: "The adulteration of food is carried on under our eyes, at our very doors, and we are so used to it that we say nothing. They put fuchsine in our wine, margarine in our butter, chicory in our coffee, tallow in our chocolate, and we swallow it all in perfect good humor. What is the use of protesting? So things are, and 'business could not be carried on' if they gave us really pure food. So we swallow it all without gagging or moving a muscle. Provided we are not poisoned—too quickly—we profess ourselves satisfied."

Everyone knows that the adulteration of food is enormous. If anyone has any doubts let him read the reports of the chemists upon a product whose adulteration is easy, milk, for example. His doubts will disappear rapidly; at least half of the milk is adulterated. It is only the adulteration of food products that constitutes a legal offense, but the adulteration of other articles does not differ from this when considered from a sociological point of view, and it is unnecessary to say that there too the adulteration is enormous.

There are, to be sure, manufacturers and merchants who are not guilty of such acts; first, because certain articles cannot be adulterated; second, because in certain branches the oversight in the interests of the consumers is very rigorous; third, because certain producers find it more advantageous to be honest, knowing that thereby they will procure a large body of regular customers. These three reasons have nothing moral in them, though there is a fourth reason which affects certain producers, namely that they have scruples against such practices.

* * *

We come now to the last category of the criminals of this group, to the great criminals, to those who throw themselves into gigantic enterprises while knowing beforehand that these will certainly or probably fail, or those who make great purchases of stock, and afterward cause a rise in price through the dissemination of false news, etc.

If there is any kind of crime that is the consequence of the economic environment exclusively, this is the one. Such crimes can arise only in a time like ours, with its insatiable thirst for gold, with the unlimited opportunity to deceive the public, greedy for great profits. A superficial knowledge of economic history is enough to make it plain that the bourgeois crimes, and especially those which we are now discussing, can be committed only under an economic system of the kind that ours is.

This should make those anthropologists reflect who wish always to find the causes of crime in the man himself and not in his surroundings. Naturally the originators of such deeds are marked out by characteristic traits. But there is no reason to admit that persons with such dispositions could not have been born also under a different economic system. Yet such crimes do not appear under any other mode of production.

What is the kind of persons who commit these crimes which society has prepared for? We note first that chance must have prepared such individuals in the proper environment, for a crime of this kind. If they were in the class of agriculturists, for example, the idea of committing it would not have occurred to them; it is only in a special environment that such crimes can be committed.

These people are characterized, in the first place, by excessive cupidity. In this regard they come high in the curve. Their prodigality is without limits; once they have executed a great coup they buy splendid palaces, give costly fêtes, support several mistresses, etc. An individual of this type, Arton, had a mistress who cost him 300,000 francs in one year; he needed a million to cover his annual expenses. This is why they are not content with the large incomes which they could obtain honestly; they wish to surpass others in wealth, being ordinarily very vain.

We have said that such individuals would probably have succeeded in securing large incomes honestly, for all are of a high order of intelligence. In following their machinations we are astonished by their perspicacity and their cleverness. Plans like theirs could never have been conceived and still less executed by men of mediocre intelligence.

*   *   *

In the third place, this class consists of persons who, as to the intensity of their moral sentiments, take the lowest place. What an ordinary criminal does in a small way, they do on a gigantic scale; while the former injures a single person, or only a few, the latter bring misfortune to great numbers. And they do it with indifference, for the disapprobation of honest men does not touch them.

As I have already shown elsewhere, brought up in no matter what environment, such individuals would not excel in the strength of their social sentiments. But I have added that, nevertheless, the influence of the environment of these persons is very great. We do not know much of the circumstances under which they have passed their youth. At least Laschi makes no mention of them in "Le crime financier," the principal work upon this class of misdeeds. It is more than probable that their moral education is totally lacking, or has been only very superficial. Theresa Humbert, for example, had already been instructed by her father in the art of swindling on a large scale.

On the other hand we know the environment in which they have generally passed the rest of their lives. They belong to the world of speculation, an environment which has very special ideas upon economic morals. In most of the cases of this kind, facts are brought out which show that the moral ideas in these circles differ much from those of the rest of mankind. It is evident that those who commit these crimes go farther than the morality of their world permits. But it takes great moral perspicacity to distinguish in this field the demarcations between what is permitted and what is not, and it is just this perspicacity that some persons lack. This is why most criminals of this kind, when they are brought into court, say with sincere conviction that they are innocent, that they have done nothing that is incompatible with morality.

Then, speculation, etc. is one of the infallible means for killing all social sentiments; it is egoism pure and simple. Can we be astonished that some of these individuals in such an environment enter into conflict with the penal law? It seems to me not. Nor is there any reason to grant that they are abnormal from a biological point of view. So even the Italian school is forced to admit that the stigmata found elsewhere cannot be pointed out in these individuals. Furthermore, in this case we can hardly speak of atavism. It may be that our ancestors were great offenders, but it is not probable that they ever were guilty of swindles of this kind.

It is not necessary to speak fully of the reasons which cause these acts to be classed as crimes. They are harmful to the regular progress of capitalism and consequently are threatened with penalties. The punishment of the adulteration of food-stuffs, on the contrary, is a consequence of the opposition of the consumers to one of the harmful effects of this system.

In this connection it is interesting to note, first, that the penalties prescribed for these crimes are relatively light as compared with those for ordinary economic crimes, like theft, for example, especially when we reflect that the harm done by them is much greater; second, that the number of punishable acts is very limited as compared with those which really deserve punishment. As Baccaro observes in his work, "Genesi e funzione delle leggi penali," it is these crimes which show clearly the class character of the penal law.

III
Sexual Crimes

Most authors who treat of the correlation between criminality and economic conditions, have devoted their attention to economic crimes especially, and have had little or nothing to say about sexual crimes. Man's sexual instincts, they say, have nothing to do with the economic life, they are a factor apart, and accordingly there is no relation between criminal sexuality and economic conditions.

We flatter ourselves that we shall be able to show that their opinion is erroneous, that a relation between sexual criminality and economic conditions does exist, although it is by nature less direct than that between economic crimes and the mode of production.

Having already remarked that the social forms of the sexual life (marriage and prostitution) are, in the last analysis, determined by the mode of production, we will not return to this topic. And it does not fall within the province of this work to speak of the relation of the intensity of the sexual life in general to economic conditions. From history we see that the sexual life plays now a greater, now a smaller part. It would be hard to admit that the causes of these changes are within man and not outside of him, particularly when very evident causes are to be found in the environment. Who does not see that the intensity of the sexual life of the upper classes of Rome of the decadence is explained by the exaggerated luxury, the idle existence of this group, and the dependent position of a part of the women (slaves).

In our present society the relation between the sexual life and economic conditions is equally clear. Everyone knows that the sexuality which occupies a very great place in that part of the bourgeoisie which passes its life in idleness and prodigality, is the consequence of this manner of living. On the other hand the low intellectual condition of the proletariat is the cause of a sexual life much more intense than it would be if the environment permitted a harmonious development of the whole nature. Engels, in his "Condition of the Working-class in England," says of the English proletarians, what is applicable to the workers in other countries also. "Next to intemperance in the enjoyment of intoxicating liquors, one of the principal faults of English working-men is sexual license. But this, too, follows with relentless logic, with inevitable necessity out of the position of a class left to itself, with no means of making use of its freedom. The bourgeoisie has left the working-class only these two pleasures, while imposing upon it a multitude of labors and hardships, and the consequence is that the working-men, in order to get something out of life, concentrate their whole energy upon these two enjoyments, carry them to excess, surrender to them in the most unbridled manner."

Further the dependent economic position of woman in our present society is also a factor of the increase in the intensity of the sexual life (especially prostitution).

However, it is not this question but sexual criminality upon which we must fix our attention. Here also we must divide the crimes into groups, as they differ too much among themselves to be treated of together. We shall take up in order, then: A. Adultery; B. Rape and indecent assault upon adults; C. Rape and indecent assault upon children.

A. Adultery

It has been said, "the history of property is also that of theft." In the same way we may say that the history of monogamy is also that of adultery, or in other words, that there is no monogamy without adultery. There must be, therefore, powerful and constant causes occasioning this offense. As we have seen above, when we were setting forth briefly the history of marriage, adultery by the man was a permitted act at different stages of the social development. If we ask why men committed this permitted act, but one reason can be alleged; *they are not monogamous by nature.* On the part of the woman the same act constituted, on the other hand, most often a very serious offense, threatened with the most severe penalties, which did not, however, prevent adultery on her side also. The cause is not different for the two sexes; women, too, are not monogamous by nature, though perhaps more nearly so than men.

From what we have just said the etiology of this crime is fixed. The only difference between the present and the past is that adultery by the man also is punished in our time—there is no change in the etiology of the crime. It may be said that the fundamental cause of adultery is to be found in the nature of man, then, and that it is thus anthropological and not social. I cannot admit this view of the matter any more than I can believe that the ultimate cause of theft is the necessity of eating in order to live. If the fundamental cause of the offense of which we are treating is to be found *in* man, it would be present always and everywhere *without reference to the environment.* Sociology shows however, that this is not so. Up to a certain degree of social development men and women alike have been free in this respect; in other cases it is only the woman who is forced to remain true to her husband; and at times both have been compelled to remain faithful. Consequently, for one who does not consider society as an immovable body, but sees that everything is in motion, the fundamental cause of this crime is to be found in the structure of society itself, which in certain cases, prohibits a man from satisfying his natural inclinations. When the polygamous tendencies are stronger than the pressure of society a crime is committed.

If we consulted only the criminal statistics we should hardly ever meet with adultery. It is unnecessary to add that the penal laws dealing with this matter are so drawn up that a prosecution for adultery almost never takes place; it goes without saying, however, that in reality the offense is very common.

In the first place we must look into the question of the classes of society in which the offense occurs oftenest. Though there are no statistics on the matter I believe that we shall not be far wrong in saying that adultery takes place oftenest in that part of the bourgeoisie that lives in idleness, often also among the proletariat, and least often among the intellectual bourgeoisie and the petty bourgeoisie. In seeking for the causes of this fact we see clearly that they cannot be found in the man himself, for the individuals forming these classes do not differ as to their innate characteristics. Consequently, these causes must be found in the environment; the following being the principal ones.

First. The more marriage is contracted for convenience the greater the danger of adultery. This is one reason why adultery is more common among the "upper ten thousand," where marriage is often a commercial affair, and why it is less frequent among the intellectual bourgeoisie, in which there are more marriages of inclination.

Second. The more frivolous and trifling the life any class leads, the more frequent will adultery be in it. This is another reason why adultery is frequent among the idle rich, and less frequent in the intellectual class and the petty bourgeoisie.

Third. The more the social causes of marriage are felt in a certain class, the greater the moral aversion to adultery. This is one reason why this offense is found less often among the petty bourgeoisie than in the working class.

Fourth. The greater the number of marriages concluded for purely physical reasons without any intellectual reasons entering in, the more numerous will be the cases of adultery. This applies especially to the proletariat, among whom most of the marriages are contracted from affection, but where, because of lack of culture, there is often no possibility of intellectual communion. When this harmony is lacking it comes about that the difficulties of life, so great in this class, cause an estrangement from which infidelities frequently result.

Finally, let us consider briefly the question of which individuals in the different classes are guilty of adultery. The predisposition to polygamy is not the same for all. In the second place, the sexual instincts are much more intense in some cases than in others. In the third place the environment in which one has lived is not the same as that of another, and opportunities do not occur in the same way for each. The joint action of these causes explains sufficiently why one commits the offense in question and not another.

In setting forth the etiology of adultery we have been giving the reasons why it has been designated as a crime. Little by little the conception of marriage has been modified in consequence of the social changes that have taken place; there is a growing number of persons who consider the life in common permissible only when both parties desire it without being constrained by the law. The partisans of this opinion disapprove of adultery, but for different reasons from others, who consider it as the infraction of an acquired right. Professor Ferri formulates this new morality as follows. "What is vile about adultery is not that it is an assault upon individual property, it is the disloyalty of the act, the trickery and hypocrisy of it."

While finding adultery immoral the adherents of this opinion believe that the law has no right to interfere. Even the persons who do not share their point of view believe that the penal code should cease to concern itself with this crime. Hence it comes, among other things, that the laws are so drawn that prosecutions are very rare. It is probable that adultery will disappear from the list of offenses.

B. Rape and Indecent Assault upon Adults

In his work, "Genèse normale du crime," Professor Manouvrier expresses himself as follows upon the crime of rape. "Every normally constituted man would be a born violator if the sexual appetite could find no other means of satisfaction than rape. The crime is rare, however, and we know why; there are women for the ugliest and the poorest. However, famine may come; there is also opportunity, and many devils capable of leading into temptation the brute that every man is at his birth. For the 'criminologists' must not delude themselves upon this point if they wish to make criminal anthropology truly scientific. If we were to take a well-born child of a distinguished European family, and isolate him from his birth from all the influences of environment except those strictly necessary for the preservation of his life, we do not know what strange beast he would turn into. On the other hand we do know that behind our acquired polish our natural brutality still persists." Here in a few words is the environment theory applied to the origin of the most serious sexual crimes. Let us consult some facts to see whether the theory is correct.

First of all it must be remarked that this crime is not the act of a pervert but of a brute. It is important not to forget this since perversion does play a part in the crimes which we shall take up under C. Some authors do not make a distinction between these two kinds of crimes, which prevents their giving a really fundamental treatment of the etiology of them.

Let us see what the movement of this crime teaches. Its curve in the different months shows that it rises towards spring, to reach its maximum in summer, after which it regularly decreases, reaching its minimum in winter.

       ❖   ❖   ❖

The movement of sexual crimes does not tell us much about their etiology. It is plain that the opportunity of committing them occurs much oftener in summer than in winter, and the chance of catching the criminal "in flagrante delicto" is also much greater during the hot months. Even without statistics we should know that the temptation to these acts is greater in warm weather, and further, the rise of temperature towards spring probably increases the sexual tendencies. But all this does not explain the origin of this class of crimes, for if it is true that the sexual tendencies in man are increased by the rise of temperature toward spring, this affects the sexual life *in general*, and not the *sexual criminality* alone. . . .

In the same way we learn little of the etiology of these crimes from their movement in the course of the years.

       ❖   ❖   ❖

The data upon the relation between the economic situation and these crimes are not as numerous as those upon economic crimes, and there are also many exceptions. With some reservations, however, we can say that an improvement in economic conditions tends to increase the crimes in question. However, this does not teach us much with regard to the etiology of them; the statistics of births have long since shown us that the sexual life is more intense during the periods of economic prosperity, than during those of depression. Better nourishment renders the sexual instincts stronger, without its being necessary that they should manifest themselves in a criminal manner. The proof of this is furnished by those who are sufficiently nourished both in good times and bad and are yet not guilty of these crimes. . . .

We must then try to discover the true crime-producing factors in other statistical data. First let us inquire whether married or unmarried persons are more often guilty? As we have seen above, German criminal statistics are the only ones which give us absolutely certain information on this point. These show . . . that at all ages bachelors, widowers, and divorced men are more often guilty of sexual crimes than married men, and at certain ages much more so. Unfortunately these statistics do not distinguish the rapes committed upon adults from those committed upon children.

*   *   *

Marriage, then, tends to diminish the number of these crimes. The economic life having, in its turn, an influence upon the number of marriages, the relation between this life and the crimes in question is clear. If the economic situation of many persons did not prevent their contracting marriage at the period of life indicated by nature, these crimes would be much less frequent. As Dr. Augagneur says: "Our laws and physiological exigencies do not harmonize."

A second question is, what is the class of the population that commits these crimes? As we have seen, the statistics of Italy and Austria show . . . that it is almost exclusively the poor who are guilty of sexual crimes. In Italy 92.1% are indigent or have only the strict necessaries of life; in Austria 91.2% are without fortune, and only 0.2% are well-to-do.

The statistics of the professions of convicts in Germany . . . show also that those who are arraigned for these crimes are especially working-men, and particularly unskilled laborers. . . . Unfortunately these statistics do not distinguish between sexual crimes committed upon adults and those committed upon children. The [data show] that the number is greater for the first than for the second of these crimes . . . [and] that the crime with which we are concerned is committed by working-people especially. The criminals in a large number of the cases are rural. . . .

* * *

Even when we take account of the fact that the rural population in France is more numerous than the urban, we still see that the crime in question is committed in the country especially.

We must further inquire what is the part of the proletariat that is guilty of rape upon adults? The answer must be that it is that which forms the lowest stratum of society. As preceding statistics have shown us . . . , the number of illiterates or of those who know only how to read and write, is very great among the authors of sexual crimes. . . . [This] crime is almost never committed by persons having more than a primary education.

This fact destroys the theory that the "human beast" exists independent of environment; for if such were the case, this crime would be relatively as frequent among more highly developed persons as among those that are less so. This . . . is always forgotten by criminal anthropologists, that a man becomes a brute only under certain fixed circumstances, and commits then acts that would be repugnant to him if he lived in a different environment.

Those who commit these acts come from the strata of society

in which, in consequence of their living conditions, the sexual life is considered from a purely animal point of view. What is the environment in which the children of the lowest classes grow up, and what is the sexual morality that they derive from it? The simple truth is that there is no sexual morality for them. In consequence of the detestable housing conditions (compare what was said upon this subject in connection with prostitution) and of the bad society with which they are thrown, the children are thoroughly conversant with the sexual life in its most bestial manifestations. Their attention is fixed upon the sexual life at an age at which it is still a closed book to children brought up in a wholesome environment. As Dr. Lux says in his excellent study upon sexual crimes, "Need, misery, and vice are the natural surroundings of the children of the proletariat, and especially of the lower proletariat; they form the environment out of which the child draws his first and most lasting impressions; they are the school from which they derive the lessons of a system of ethics which is in marked contrast with the ethics of progressive humanity. Conceptions of moral restraints can hardly be awakened in the offspring of the lowest ranks of the proletariat; on the contrary, so far as the sexual sphere is concerned, they are suppressed by the undisguised sexual intercourse of parents, other adults, and prostitutes, with whom the children are continually coming into contact. . . ."

One of the consequences of the lower position of woman in our present society is that man considers women as destined to submit to his sexual will. This is especially the case in the lower strata of the population, where the woman is often only a means by which the man may satisfy his desires.

Finally, alcoholism is still to be added as a criminogenic factor. Above . . . we have seen that there are many chronic alcoholics among the authors of these crimes; in Germany 23.3% and 20.5%, in France 51.5% and 55.7%, in the Netherlands 10.84%, and in Wurtemberg 36.3%.

There is still another way in which alcoholism figures in the etiology of these crimes. At a certain stage of intoxication the sexual instincts are stimulated, while the moral forces are weakened. So in the cases where a sexual crime has been committed in a state of drunkenness we may be sure that alcohol has been one of the principal factors of it.

*   *   *

To sum up, we see that the causes of these crimes are the economic condition which prevents some individuals from marrying at the natural age, the inferior social position of woman, alcoholism, and above all the sexual demoralization and lack of civilization in the lowest strata of society.

It is plain that not all the individuals who live in this environment are guilty of the crimes in question. The sexual instincts do not have equal force at all ages, nor with all individuals. There are individals who have very pronounced sexual propensities, others who are almost indifferent in this respect, and between the two extremes lies the great majority. It is only for the first class that the danger of a crime against morals is great, for the others it is less so. If the opportunity (rape is almost always an "occasional" crime) presents itself to persons already predisposed, the moral check to restrain them is lacking. If they had lived in another environment, this act would be repugnant to them, as statistics prove; for this crime is not committed by persons of the other classes, although there are naturally proportionally more persons with strong sexual instincts among them. The opportunity to commit these crimes is happily not very frequent. As Voltaire has expressed it, "Rape is a crime as hard to prove as it is to commit."

We must add a few words upon the history of this crime and the causes that have led to its being classified as such. As Dr. Post (the principal authority upon this question) has shown, among many primitive peoples rape is only considered as a detriment to the property of the man. It is only little by little as the position of woman improves, and her individuality is recognized, that rape is considered as a grave encroachment upon the liberty of the woman, and that it is punished as such.

C. Rape and Indecent Assault upon Children

An examination of the etiology of these crimes shows that in great part the individuals who are guilty of them belong to the same category of criminals as those who commit sexual crimes upon adults. If they seduce or outrage a child and not a woman it is from accidental reasons (opportunity, lack of bodily strength, etc.); they are brutes who wish to satisfy their sexual instincts at any price; they are not, however, perverts. Although there is a quantitative difference between the man who violates an adult and one who commits this act upon a child (the latter being grosser and more egoistic than the former), there is no qualitative difference between the two so far as the majority of the criminals of whom we are speaking are concerned. We should only repeat ourselves if we treated of the etiology of these crimes more fully.

As with the crimes of which we were speaking above, there is with crimes against children also, a great increase toward spring, the maximum being reached in the month of June, after which there is a decrease, with the minimum in winter. The statistics given for France show also that in this country the periods of economic prosperity bring an increase of these crimes, and the periods of depression a decrease. And it is probably the same with other countries. As has been said also of the crimes against adults, all this shows us very little of the etiology of these crimes, since the intensity of the sexual life in general rises and falls in accordance with the economic situation.

Here also the married men play a smaller part than the unmarried and divorced; the poor classes show a larger number of crimes than those that have property . . . ; the illiterate, and persons who know how to read and write simply, show also proportionately higher figures than persons with a higher education, and alcoholism again takes its place among the causes of this crime.

A minute comparison of the statistics of sexual crimes committed upon adults and of those upon children shows that a part of the latter are of a character quite different from the former. By comparing, for example, the statistics of the civil status of persons arraigned, we see that the number of married men and widowers is proportionately much greater in the case of crimes against children than against adults.

* * *

A comparison of the statistics of the occupation of the two groups of these criminals . . . shows that in the crimes upon children, the liberal professions show twice as many as those committed upon adults. The same is true of merchants.

The figures with regard to education show that the illiterate are about equally numerous in both groups of criminals, but that the percentage of those who have a higher education is 5 in the case of crimes upon children, and barely 1 for those upon adults.

While, as we have seen, sexual crimes upon adults are chiefly committed in the country, the cities and manufacturing centers occupy a much more important place in the statistics of those upon children. . . .

Contrary to what we find with regard to sexual crimes against adults it is also the departments with the great cities which, in comparison with the rural districts, give the highest figures.

It appears from an examination of these data that sexual crimes upon children and those upon adults have, in part a different etiology. Many sexual crimes upon children are committed by persons who could satisfy their desires with adults, but abuse children instead. These, then, are cases of sexual perverts.

A thorough examination of the causes of this perversion would be ill placed in the midst of our investigation of the social etiology of crime, for they are principally of a pathological nature. However prostitution should be mentioned as contributing more to sexual demoralization than any other cause.

*   *   *

It is plainly difficult to show by figures the degree of importance of prostitution in the etiology of sexual crimes. The Swiss statistics, which try, though very imperfectly, to record the causes of crimes, say that 5.3% of the sexual crimes are caused by prostitution. It is unnecessary to say that this figure is too low.

We may add in conclusion that it is almost always upon the children of the poor that these crimes are committed. The children of well-to-do parents are so well guarded that crimes against them are the rare exceptions.

IV
Crimes from Vengeance and Other Motives

Besides economic, sexual, and political criminality, there is still a fourth category of crimes, the motives of which are quite diverse. We shall treat, A. Crimes from vengeance, and B. Infanticide. The first group is important both quantitatively and qualitatively; the second, especially, qualitatively. The crimes committed from other motives are either very rare, or very insignificant, or may be explained by the same causes as those included under A, and hence may be passed over in silence.

A. Crimes Committed from Vengeance

In a sociological work like ours we need not consider the psychology of vengeance. For our subject it is sufficient to show that the feeling is innate in everyone, although in different degrees. As soon as one person injures another, whether bodily, or in his interests, or his honor, the desire to retaliate in one way or another immediately appears. If this desire transforms itself into act, this act calls forth a stronger reaction on the part of the opposing party, etc. It is this that is called the instinct of vengeance.

We must then begin by treating the causes calling forth feelings of revenge, and by fixing our attention upon the two principal categories of causes, those which spring from the economic life, and those which are due to the sexual life.

We shall speak first of the causes that are due to the economic life. The fundamental principle of the mode of production in which we live is competition, strife—in other words, doing injury to others. So there are innumerable cases in which the desire for revenge is excited by the economic life. Many sociologists extol the beauty of this struggle and pretend that its effect upon society is excellent. We shall refrain from examining the truth or falsity of this statement; for the matter in hand we need not concern ourselves with the fortunate victors, but simply with the vanquished. After the exposition of the present system of production it is superfluous to show all the opposing economic interests and the feelings resulting therefrom; we shall mention a few, and the other will be easily understood.

Imagine, for example, the state of mind of a small retailer who finds himself totally ruined by the competition of a large department store in the neighborhood; of that of workingmen suffering great privations during a strike, who see themselves supplanted by others, who think only of their immediate interest in acting as strike-breakers. Or imagine, again, the innumerable cases in which questions of inheritance awaken vengeful feelings. And side by side with all this, picture the economic life of village-communities where all the economic interests were parallel, and where consequently the economic life engendered neither envy nor jealousy. Anyone who grasps the enormous difference between these two modes of production, will understand also how the feelings of revenge are excited by the present economic system.

In the second place, how far are vengeful feelings aroused by sexuality? As Sutherland remarks in his "Origin and Growth of the Moral Instinct," there are no peoples who are not more or less jealous in sexual matters, but great differences are to be observed in this respect. While Nansen, for example tells how the Eskimo women are almost ignorant of sexual jealousy, there are other peoples among whom the woman is killed by her husband if another man evinces any regard for her.

The facts show that the greater the power of the man over the woman, the greater also is the sexual jealousy of the man, a jealousy which, among other things, manifests itself in the very severe punishment of adultery. He who has a right to something wishes to keep it for himself and does not tolerate injury to it on the part of anyone else. When the man considers the woman as his chattel, or when he has great power over her, sexual jealousy is strengthened by the feelings connected with property. These latter feelings were more predominant among the primitive peoples than true sexual jealousy, a proof of which is that fact that among many of these peoples the law of hospitality required putting the wife at the disposal of the guest.

From the present form of marriage (as among many primitive peoples) it follows that each party has a right with relation to the other. The violation of this right is considered as a serious injury and gives rise to a desire for revenge. This phenomenon is not natural, but historical. If the present state of society did not necessitate an artificial stability in sexual relationships, if the man and his wife were economically independent, they would not believe that they had rights over each other.

Here is the first bond between sexual jealousy and the social environment, but there is also a second, though a more remote one, namely, that it is with those who have a gross conception of the relations of man and wife, that revengeful feelings arise after love disappears. Those who, because of the environment in which they live, have formed a different idea of the relation between man and wife, while feeling the most violent grief, remain strangers to the desire for revenge. He who knows that neither love nor sympathy can be bidden, knows also that a right in this matter can bring no change in action of fate, where the brute sees an evil will. This is one reason why the number of crimes of passion is smaller among civilized people than among the partly civilized.

We must notice, further, one kind of crime of passion, the revenge of a woman seduced and then abandoned. Besides sexual jealousy there are, in these cases, other motives playing their part. Often the women has not given herself for love alone, but also with the prospect of a marriage, or a betterment of her economic position. It is not sexual vengeance that is the sole motive here then, but also vengeance for economic reasons. Further the prohibition of inquiring into the question of paternity may also enter in.

After having pointed out the two principal categories of causes that awaken revengeful feelings we must now enquire why, with certain individuals, these feelings are translated into acts. Many criminologists prefer to find environment of small importance in these crimes and the individual factors the predominant ones. Let us see whether the facts will uphold this theory. To begin with let us ask what the movement of these crimes teaches us.

As statistics show, they increase towards spring, reach their maximum in summer, after which a decrease follows with the minimum in winter.

❂   ❂   ❂

Some authors seek for a remote explanation, when there is one near at hand: in summer persons are more in contact with each other, a fact which gives opportunity for disputes, and an increased danger of consequent crimes.

We may sum up the principal data upon the movement of these crimes in relation to the economic situation. . . .

*   *   *

Examining these results we observe that the crimes in question increase in the periods of prosperity, and vice versa; but we see at the same time that there are also noteworthy exceptions (New South Wales and France), and that in Germany in the last 20 or 30 years, this tendency is no longer present. It is not difficult, it seems to me, to explain why these crimes increase in periods of prosperity. Men are thrown then into contact more frequently, they live a little more for amusement, and consume (and this is certainly one of the principal reasons) more alcohol than usual. Some authors see in this movement of crimes against persons a natural law, according to which criminality would be a fixed quantity, manifesting itself in economic crimes in periods of depression, and in crimes against the person in periods of prosperity.

As I have already said more than once this theory is erroneous. If it were really true that an improvement of the economic situation *inevitably* brought about an increase of crimes against persons, the class of individuals who are always in fairly good circumstances would also be largely guilty of these crimes. Statistics show us the contrary.

Thus we arrive at the very important question, what are the classes of the population which are especially guilty of these crimes? As the statistics already given show they are the poorest classes. . . . In Italy, for example, 89.8% of those who commit homicide, and 91.1% of those guilty of assault, were indigent or had only the bare necessities of life, though these form but 60% of the population. The same is true of Austria, and the statistics of occupations give a similar result for Germany. . . .

The statistics that give information upon the degree of education of these criminals are more interesting still. As we have seen above, only 0.1% of those guilty of assault had a higher education, while 40.5% of these criminals were illiterate, and 59.4% knew only how to read, or to read and write. In France from 1896 to 1900 the completely illiterate constituted 16% of those guilty of assault, and 15% of the assassins, while in the general population there were only 4.5% who did not know how to sign their names. In Italy only 1% of the assassins and only 0.6% of those guilty of assault had a higher education, 99% and 99.4% respectively were illiterate or knew only how to read and write. These are striking figures.

In this connection let us stop for a moment to consider the geography of these crimes, and place beside the figures on this point those of illiteracy.

*   *   *

In view of all the preceding data we must conclude that it is the less civilized persons who commit crimes of this class. How is this to be explained? This is what we shall proceed to examine.

The first reason is that the more civilized a person is, the less revengeful feelings arise when some one injures him. The more the motives of actions are appreciated, the less the desire for revenge springs up. A child wants to revenge himself even upon an inanimate object that has hurt him; it is almost the same with uncivilized peoples, who so rarely take account of the motives of human action. It is not so long ago that men took vengeance upon maniacs, a thing which could not happen today.

In the second place, when the idea of revenge arises in a civilized man he is more in a position to restrain himself than the uncivilized; he is less impulsive; he knows that later he will repent of his act, and that it may have disagreeable consequences for him.

In the third place civilization inspires a great aversion to acts of violence.

Thus we come to the correlation between these crimes and

the education of the poor. The child is often moved to revenge; there is no inner check to restrain his passions. When his education has been neglected he runs, as his age advances, more danger than others of being guilty of these crimes. And then children are very imitative. If we had good statistics with regard to violent criminals we should see that they almost always spring from surroundings in which violence is common. All authors who are especially concerned with this matter are in agreement on this point. The fact that parents among the lower classes use blows as a means of instruction has for its national consequence that when the children are grown they themselves have no fear of making use of violence.

One further observation must be made here. Many persons think it quite natural that one should not have the right to avenge himself for an injury. Sociology, however, teaches us quite otherwise. Among primitive peoples revenge, instead of being a thing prohibited, is a sacred duty. Little by little vengeance, at first unlimited, became confined to "an eye for an eye, a tooth for a tooth"; this in turn was replaced by the so called "composition"; and this in its turn yielded to penalties inflicted by an authority superior to both parties.

If we enquire which are the countries where homicides and assaults are committed most frequently, we find that they are the most backward, and thus give a picture of time past. Here we have in mind especially Sicily . . . and Corsica (while between 1880 and 1884 there was an annual average [in Italy] of 6.4 homicides to the million inhabitants, the figure for homicides in Corsica was 110.2). Nothing is more mistaken than to believe that we have here a question of race. [There] have been times when the people of these countries were much less violent than the northern peoples, now so little given to this kind of crime. These two islands have so high a figure because the "vendetta" is still universal there, and because it is considered as a duty.

Although in less degree, the case is almost the same with the lower classes of other countries as regards this type of crime. There are those who from their manner of life most resemble our distant ancestors. They are not, at least so much as other classes of society, instilled with the idea that they have no right to avenge themselves personally. On the contrary it is often considered an act of cowardice to allow an insult or an injury to pass without taking revenge. This is why the police are often resisted and their interference considered as an intrusive meddling with matters with which they have no concern.

Such, in my opinion, are the principal reasons why the less civilized classes are guilty of these crimes, and thus we are given an idea of their etiology.

In the first table upon the relation between illiteracy and serious assaults (Germany) we added also the percentage of votes given to the socialists. As the table shows the percentage of these votes is in general smaller in the localities where the kind of crime of which we have been treating is most frequent; and vice versa. It is, then, evident that there is a correlation between the two phenomena, and this is easily explained. In the working circles in which socialism is beginning to make its way, there is growing little by little, an interest in things other than those which formerly occupied the working-men in their leisure hours. They begin to become civilized and to have an aversion to the coarser amusements. At the same time the feeling of solidarity is awakened in them, and thus a powerful moral check is created.

It was especially the figures for the crimes of vengeance that we placed beside . . . the votes given to the socialists, since the relation between the two phenomena stands out very distinctly. This correlation, however, holds for criminality in general, for almost all the countries with a large number of socialist voters show also fairly low figures for criminality, and vice versa. Nevertheless this correlation is not as great for other crimes as for those which we are at present considering, which is explained by the fact that most of the criminals who are guilty of them are not much like other criminals, especially those who have no respect for property (criminals from poverty excepted). These last, greedy of pleasure, and always looking out for their own interests, are those who, as regards the intensity of their social instincts, occupy the last place. All this is inapplicable to criminals by violence; they are not always really wicked, and after their crime they often show a sincere repentance. Socialism exercises no influence upon the category of individuals from whom the economic criminals (from cupidity) are recruited, persons, that is to say, who think only of their own interest, and show themselves insensible to a movement for the well-being of the whole working class.

We have still to speak of one question which is sometimes put in treating of this subject. If it is true, says some one, that it is principally in consequence of their ignorance and their lack of civilization that the lower classes commit the crimes in question, these crimes must little by little present themselves less often, for the development of these classes is improving, even if only gradually. Now criminal statistics do show a gradual diminution in these crimes. Homicide, the gravest form, has continually decreased in England, Switzerland, France, and Sweden (where it has been reduced to a very small figure), and in Italy (where a considerable diminution has been shown). If we had criminal statistics much more ancient than the existing ones it would be shown that this crime has decreased enormously compared with remote epochs. The progress of civilization in the lower strata of society is very slow, and criminal statistics are all of relatively recent date.

Germany is, as far as I know, the only country where there has been any considerable increase in these crimes (except those against life) in the last twenty years. This exception does not, in my opinion, invalidate the rule. The lack of civilization among the lower orders is not the sole cause of these crimes; the innumerable conflicts engendered by the present social system are also a cause. Besides, the impulse given by the economic development in Germany during this period has hardly been equalled in other countries; it has seen its population grow and become congested, and conflicts increase in like proportion, a cause sufficient to neutralize the civilization which brings it about. Further there is the possibility that the police and the courts have been more efficient during this period, so as to make the increase of crime seem greater than it really is. Finally, alcoholism is increasing, and may also neutralize the effect of civilization.

We come, then, to one of the most important causes of this kind of crime, namely alcoholism. Not only is chronic alcoholism demoralizing . . . but drunkenness at the acute stage makes a person more disposed to commit acts of violence, and at the same time less able to control his instincts and passions. Further, the degree of civilization reached by the individual has a great influence upon his conduct when he is intoxicated; the civilized man is then much less dangerous than the man without education. Dr. Grotjahn puts it as follows: "The development of the moral consciousness is not without influence upon the harmlessness or danger of intoxication. Persons in whom the sense of responsibility for the consequences of their actions has been sharpened by education, whether they owe this to their teachers or their parents or to their own experience, in case they become intoxicated to the point of having their minds clouded, will still always keep a remnant of their power of judgment, which will hold them back from violent and disastrous actions. On the other hand, in the case of persons who lack all moral training, the scanty moral restraints which check their native impulses most quickly disappear."

An examination of the physiological process caused by large doses of alcohol not coming properly within the scope of a sociological work like this, it is sufficient to show that great quantities of alcohol undoubtedly do have this effect. We shall accordingly pass on to the question of the correlation between violent crime and the acute stage of alcoholism.

There are different ways of attempting to settle this question. [We] have seen that some authors have tried the dynamic method, Fornasari di Verce, for example, showing that in Italy, Great Britain, Ireland, and New South Wales, these crimes increase and diminish with the consumption of alcohol. Professor Ferri shows that during the years 1849–1880 the increase and diminution of cases of assault in France coincide with the success and failure of the vintage.

Another method consists in inquiring what day of the week assaults are most frequent. If the abuse of alcohol is really an important factor in the etiology of these crimes more of them must be committed upon Sunday, Saturday, and Monday, for the abuse of alcohol is greatest on these days.

*   *   *

The figures and the thesis agree, then, perfectly. It is plain, to be sure, that we cannot charge all the cases falling on Sunday to alcohol, since people come together more on that day, and hence the danger of a conflict is greater, but most of the Sunday cases are certainly due to alcohol.

Other authors compare the geography of these crimes with the consumption of alcohol. Professor Aschaffenburg, for example, . . . points out the fact that in Germany the countries with the greatest number of assaults are also those where there is the largest consumption of alcohol.

However, although these indirect methods are not without value, it seems to me that since they contain so many elements of uncertainty they yield to the direct method. It is for this reason that I shall follow here especially the direct method and shall indicate the percentage of those who have committed these crimes when they were in a state of intoxication. Though making use of this direct method I do not think it infallible, but it is less liable to error than the others. The especial weakness of it is that the persons who are accused pretend in extenuation that they committed their crimes in a state of drunkenness. Good statistics do not rely solely upon the statements of the prisoners, but also upon the facts brought out at the trial. And then, as Professor Löffler remarks, all those arraigned are not acute enough to simulate a state of drunkenness, and there are even those who, although addicted to overindulgence in alcohol, will deny that they were intoxicated, either from shame, or for fear of a more severe punishment.

Most criminal statistics do not concern themselves with this subject, and even those that do are less detailed than we might wish. Nevertheless they are sufficient, I believe, to prove the correlation in question.

*   *   *

We have now reached the end of our remarks upon the etiology of these crimes, and have shown that the principal causes are, first, the present structure of society, which brings about innumerable conflicts; second, the lack of civilization and education among the poorer classes; and third, alcoholism, which is in turn a consequence of the social environment.

What part is played in these crimes by the so-called individual factors? It seems to me that it is like that which the individual factors play in other crimes—they explain in part which are the individuals that commit the crimes, but they do not explain why the crimes are committed.

This is totally contrary to what many criminologists claim, namely that it is especially the effect of individual factors that is seen in these crimes. Statistics prove the inaccuracy of this. If it were true, these crimes ought to appear equally in all classes of society, which, as we have seen, is not the case. A choleric person naturally runs more danger of committing such a crime than one who is phlegmatic; but no one will deny that in all classes the proportion of the persons born with a choleric disposition is the same. However, the influence of environment brings it about that in the well-to-do classes even the choleric run little danger of such a crime. Superficial civilization (for a veneer is all that a great part of the bourgeoisie possesses) is sufficient to limit these crimes to an insignificant minimum.

The obviousness of the reasons which have caused these acts to be classed as crimes is such that it is needless to speak of them. In a society like ours, with its numerous conflicts and its dense population, life would be impossible if the individual were not forbidden to avenge himself personally. Sociology teaches us that vengeance, at first permitted, and even obligatory, has become a prohibited act, because of the great harm it does to society

B. Infanticide

There are two chief motives for infanticide, which operate separately or together, namely, fear of dishonor, and poverty. We shall speak first of the former and put the question to begin with, what sort of persons are guilty of this crime? Criminal statistics answer that—

First, they are, almost without exception, women.

Second, they are unmarried women much oftener than married.

Third, the guilty are almost exclusively very poor. According to Italian statistics 88.1% of them are indigent; in Austria, 90.8%; and there are no rich or well-to-do women among them.

Fourth, the women of the working class are much more often guilty than those of the independent class, and the class of domestics furnishes especially a very high figure (Germany). These results are confirmed by the data of other countries. In Austria 80% of those convicted between 1880 and 1882 were domestics, and in France the same was true of 35% of those convicted between 1876 and 1880.

Fifth, the women working in the fields are especially likely to fall into this crime (Germany); the data of other countries also show that it is especially in the country that infanticide is committed. Dr. Socquet shows that in France between 1871 and 1875 there were, to the million inhabitants, 35 persons arraigned out of the rural population, and 22 to the urban.

Sixth, illiteracy is very frequent among those convicted of infanticide. We have seen that in Austria 39.5%, in France 20.0%, and in Italy 92.9% were illiterate. Women knowing more than how to read and write were not found among these criminals.

Most of the cases of infanticide are identical; it generally is, as Fournier says, "a girl who has allowed herself to have a child without the permission of the municipality," and who has been abandoned by her lover.

The ruling moral ideas place before her a frightful dilemma; if her pregnancy is known by those about her and the child remains alive, she is covered with ignominy, and a painful life awaits her. On the other hand if she makes the child disappear, the others ignore everything, and she avoids dishonor and its consequences. She therefore attempts to conceal her pregnancy as long as possible, in the hope of a miscarriage. But when she finds herself disappointed, when not only terrible physical pains, but also mental tortures are making her almost mad—then it happens that she kills her child.

Statistics show that most of these crimes are committed by women of the lower classes. The number of unmarried mothers is here relatively great; infanticide is quite rare (though a little more frequent than one would suppose from the criminal statistics). There must be special circumstances, therefore, to lead some of these women to this crime. As we have seen in treating of marriage, the ideas of intimate relations between persons who are not married are much less severe in the proletariat, than in the bourgeoisie (a consequence of the fact that the social causes of marriage are much less strong in the latter than in the former), so that among the proletariat these relations are pretty common. If they have consequences, the father and mother generally marry. In this case the idea of killing the child does not come to the women. The unmarried mothers (very often domestics), who are guilty of this crime are especially those who, seduced and then abandoned by men of a higher class, have no family that can receive them.

Besides women of the working class, there are also among the infanticides some of the petty bourgeoisie, where the moral disapproval of extra-matrimonial sexual commerce is very severe.

Not all women who find themselves in the situation described commit the crime in question, of course. One will reason more than another, and will prefer dishonor to the danger of a criminal trial; one woman has the maternal instinct more fully developed than another, etc. In relation to the social sentiments we see here a situation contrary to what occurs in the case of most crimes. Crime is an egoistic act, that is to say an act which injures the interests of others. This is true of infanticide, but this differs from most of the other crimes in being committed to escape moral disapproval, while they are committed only to obtain a personal profit or to satisfy the passions. This is why those guilty of infanticide are not generally those whose social sentiments have little intensity, as is mostly the case with those who are guilty of economic or sexual crimes. Infanticides are persons sensitive to the opinions of others, while those who have little social feeling easily bear shame.

These individual differences explain in part which are the individuals who become guilty of the crime in question, but not the cause of its existence. There are only a few crimes whose social origin is as clear as that of infanticide. If the present structure of society did not make the present form of marriage necessary, and thus bring about moral disapprobation of extra-matrimonial sexual relations, there would be no infanticide caused by fear of dishonor.

The repression of some of the strongest *natural* desires, required by our present *society*, is so great that these requirements are bound to be violated by some individuals in whom these desires are very pronounced. This is true not only in the sphere of the economic life, but also in that of the sexual life. As long as cupidity is awakened in many, while only a few can satisfy it, theft will exist; as long as the satisfaction of the sexual desires is permitted only after certain economic conditions have been complied with, the prohibition will be violated, and some persons will try to destroy the evidence of their acts.

Besides the fear of shame, poverty also plays a part in the etiology of infanticide. Again, it is the two motives combined that are responsible. The great number of infanticides among domestics are not committed simply from fear of shame, but also because the mother, abandoned by everyone (especially in a country where inquiry into paternity is prohibited) does not know how to support her child. Besides these cases there are some committed from poverty alone, for example when married women commit this crime (something, it should be added, which happens very rarely).

Some statistical data will show that poverty is a fairly important factor in the etiology of infanticide. Dr. Weiss shows that in *Belgium* infanticide increased greatly in the years that were bad economically . . ., and Dr. Starke does the same for *Prussia.* . . .

As we have pointed out above, infanticide for the cause of poverty was quite general among primitive peoples, since they were not in a position to support a large population. It was for this reason that the act was not considered immoral, and that it was even required in some cases. In consequence of the continually increasing productivity of labor, infanticide fell more and more into desuetude, and at the same time was considered more and more reprehensible.

V
Political Crimes

Finally we have still to treat of political offenses, offenses which, in comparison with others, occur very rarely, and which by their nature are totally different.

The origin of the state, and the possibility of political crimes, are bound up with a certain phase of the development of the economic life, that is to say with the origin of marked contrasts of fortune. Those who had monopolized the power in the state defended their position by laws whose infraction was threatened with severe penalties. Economic conditions, however, undergo considerable changes, and when these have reached a certain degree, the oppressed class, having become the more powerful, breaks the political power of the ruling class and seizes it for itself. If the dominant class does all that it can to maintain its position unimpaired to the last moment, it will necessarily happen that this development will lead to political crimes. This kind of political crime may be called great political criminality. In western Europe the last great struggle of this nature was that of the feudal classes and the bourgeoisie. The former, once necessary, had become superfluous and harmful; the bourgeoisie on the other hand, from an insignificant class had become the most important. It overturned the whole political system which embarrassed it, seized the power, and transformed the state according to the exigencies of the economic system. A repetition of the same process in eastern Europe we are now witnessing in the changes going on in Russia. The economic development no longer corresponds to the political system, which sooner or later will inevitably be replaced by the modern system.

It would be a waste of time to insist upon the fact that those who commit these acts have nothing in common with ordinary criminals but the name. Most criminals are individuals whose social sentiments are reduced to a minimum, and who injure others purely for the satisfaction of their own desires. The political criminals of whom we are speaking, on the other hand, are the direct opposite; they risk their most sacred interests, their liberty and their life, for the benefit of society; they injure the ruling class only to aid the oppressed classes, and consequently all humanity. While the ordinary criminal is generally "l'homme canaille" . . . , the political criminal is "homo nobilis." History rights the matter, for the name of the ordinary great criminal is pronounced only with horror, and ends by falling into oblivion, while the political criminal survives in the memory of posterity as a hero.

We must put in the same class the political criminals who aim to deliver a subjugated people from their oppressors. The authors of these crimes also have nothing in common with ordinary criminals.

Besides these two kinds of political crimes, which are plainly collective in their nature, there are cases of crimes committed by individuals which for the most part are attempts upon the life of the monarch or of one of his representatives. The more absolute a government, the more liberty is restricted, and the less chance there is, consequently, of seeing the situation changed by legal means, the greater will become the danger that one of those oppressed will kill the autocrat, either to better the situation or to take revenge for what he and his have suffered. Anyone who wants to follow the genesis of this kind of crime has only to turn to Russia. There all the factors meet which lead to political homicide; the repression of all freedom, a corrupt bureaucracy, and the impossibility of obtaining the least change by legal means.

These circumstances naturally excite the revengeful feelings which sooner or later show themselves in acts. Though we may have the conviction that these acts are almost always useless, though we may have a deep aversion to violence—this does not justify us in ranking those who do these things with ordinary criminals. It matters not how we may abhor violence as such, every reasonable man will justify it when it serves to defend oneself, and most of the acts of political criminals in Russia are only acts of defense against the unheard-of cruelty and violence of the government.

Finally there remains a third kind of political crimes, analogous to ordinary crime, the assassination of the monarch by individuals who thus attempt to place themselves in power. These are actuated by the same vile motives that inspire the robber-murderer—cupidity, desire to dominate, etc.

Now what are the political crimes committed in our days? Leaving aside the case of Russia, which is still living in an epoch that western Europe has left behind, there are only the political crimes of socialists and anarchists. There is little to be said about those committed by socialists. The international social democracy attempts to reach its end by legal means. Since the fall of absolutism it has been possible to exercise an influence on the state in this way, an influence which varies with the country. It is this possibility that the social democracy makes use of. In conformity with its fundamental principles it rejects all violence against the head of the state. Accordingly its partisans have never committed such acts. The more democratic the constitution of a country, the less justification the social democracy will have for political crimes, as in Switzerland, for example, a country where the penal code, moreover, mentions but few political crimes. In other countries, where the democratic institutions are weak, where the constitutional monarchy has still an absolutist character, and where social democracy has become powerful, as in Germany, political crimes are inevitable. Their number, however, is insignificant in comparison with ordinary crimes. From a criminological point of view they have little importance, though often punished severely, and they are generally limited to the crime of leze majesty. Social democrats are, then, sometimes guilty of minor political offenses, and in some countries only. Whether this party will not in the future be guilty of crime of the great political type, or, in other words, whether it will not come to political revolution, is another question and one that no one can answer with certainty. Like all the bourgeoisie when the contest with the feudal classes was still going on, the social democrats are a revolutionary class; they wish to place society upon a basis different from the present one. It is possible that in democratic countries they will attain this by legal means, and consequently without there being any reason for political crime. However, it may also happen that at a given moment when the proletariat forms the majority of the legislative body, the ruling class may have recourse to a "coup d'état," to a political crime, in order to prevent the proletariat from governing. This possibility is even a probability in some countries, where the opposition of classes is very marked. In Germany, for example, where the social democracy is very powerful, it is very likely that the government will attempt some day to suppress universal suffrage by a coup d'état. It is only in such a case that the social democracy will in its turn abandon the legal way and be forced to have recourse to other methods.

In the second place there are the political crimes of anarchists. Their number is not great enough for us to learn their etiology from statistics. We must therefore analyze individual cases. What are the individuals that are guilty of these? The anarchists of the propaganda are most exclusively young men. Leauthier and Langs were 20 years old, Angelillo also, Henry 21, Caserio 21, Schwabe 23, Pallas 24, Lucheni 25, Vaillant and Bresci 31, and Salvador 33, at the time they committed their crimes, and as far as I know there were none of them who were over 33. In disposition they were very excitable. As soon as an idea took hold of them they thought of nothing else. Chance brought them into contact with anarchism which immediately made a conquest of them. Brought up in another environment they would have become, for example, religious devotees; in fact Caserio, Salvador, Vaillant, Cyvoct, and Henry were such before becoming anarchists.

Extreme individualism is also a characteristic of theirs. They abhor discipline, from which it follows that they nourish a fierce hatred of militarism. Even a mild form of discipline, such as that of a party of which one voluntarily becomes a member, is insupportable to them. Some of them have been socialists, but have soon left the party. Among these was Henry, who says in his defense: "For an instant I was attracted by socialism, but I did not delay in separating myself from this party. I had too much love for liberty, too much respect for individual initiative, too much repugnance to incorporation, to take a number in the enlisted army of the fourth estate."

Another characteristic of nearly all active anarchists, and one intimately connected with the preceding, is great vanity. Lucheni, for instance, in speaking of his crime said, "I wanted to kill a person of note, because that would get into print." Vaillant had himself photographed before making his attack, distributed his portraits right and left, and when arrested asked whether the journals had printed his picture, etc.

These traits of character, observed in the case of these individuals, are not rare; vain and excitable individualists are fairly numerous, yet almost none become active anarchists. We must therefore seek the explanation elsewhere, and ask ourselves the question, in what environment have they lived? When the president of the tribunal before which Lucheni appeared, asked him what was the motive that led him to commit his act, he replied, "It was poverty." This is applicable to almost all the active anarchists. See, for example, the life of Vaillant. An illegitimate child without any education, he had to earn his living at the age of 12; having escaped from his employer, with whom he was living, he implored his mother to take him in. Rebuffed he had himself arrested by the police, but when he was once more brought back to his parents they refused anew to receive him. He tried to make his own way, but failed in all that he undertook. It was when embittered by all the miseries he had experienced that he became acquainted with socialism, but finding this too theoretical he ranked himself on the side of the anarchists, and the last link in this chain of misery was his well-known crime.

There are authors who claim that poverty is not to be considered as one of the principal causes of anarchy, and in support of their assertion cite the case of Henry and some others, who while not living in easy circumstances, yet did not know the blackest poverty. Those who reason thus have a false notion of the motives that impel anarchists. It is not only the poverty that they have themselves experienced that moves them, but also, and chiefly, the poverty of others. Those who remain insensible to the sufferings of their neighbors never become anarchists; for not being able to draw any personal profit from anarchism, they consider it madness. Placed in unfavorable conditions such persons become ordinary criminals, or commit suicide. They never sacrifice themselves for an ideal.

Thus we come to another psychological trait of the anarchists, namely that they are born with pronounced altruistic tendencies. It is their altruism which separates them from the ordinary great criminal, whose social instincts are very weak.

It seems paradoxical to say that persons who commit such acts are of an altruistic nature, but the paradox is only apparent. When two persons, an egoist and an altruist, see a child being maltreated, the former goes on his way saying that he would only get himself into trouble if he interfered; the latter, on the other hand, delivers the child from his tormentor, to whom he may give a good thrashing in addition. Here the violent person is the altruist, the other the egoist. Every comparison is imperfect, and this is the case with the one before us, but there is some analogy between the act cited and those of the anarchists. The crimes which they commit are egoistic towards certain persons, but altruistic with reference to others. As a consequence of their own poverty and of the irritation they feel when they see that of their fellows, they have been seized with a hatred of society and wish to avenge themselves. These sentiments are not tempered by much intellectual development. This is a very important factor in the development of active anarchism. Almost all these persons are either very ignorant or have only an elementary education, some know a little more, and persons of thorough education are not found at all among them. Further, most of them lack pronounced intellectual aptitudes, but are rather especially impulsive.

These individuals, excitable, vain, with little intellectual capacity, and ignorant in addition, but oppressed by their own poverty and that of others, and filled with a hatred of society, come into contact with anarchism. It is unnecessary to give an exposition of this doctrine; the active anarchists in their ignorance get no clear idea of any theory whatever, and certainly not of anything as vague and confused as anarchism. They have heard it said that it looks to the formation of a society of altruists where there will be no more poverty, and this appeals to their altruistic instincts; at the same time anarchism gives a preponderating part to the individual, and this draws their vanity. Thus their hate increases, and at the same time attaches itself to certain individuals, whom anarchism holds responsible for existing conditions. Further, the absurd opinion has been instilled into them that it is possible for society to be reorganized at a single stroke, and that to attain this end it will be necessary to use violence.

Is it astonishing that such individuals come to attempt homicide? No; to be sure all persons of this kind do not go so far; for that it would be necessary that other conditions should be complied with. It is plain that persons with a great aversion to violence would run little risk of attempting an assassination, with others it is courage that is lacking; others still attach too high a price to life and liberty to be willing to risk them; etc. We must note this last point especially. Generally active anarchists are persons who care nothing for a life in which they have nothing further to lose. Their conduct in court and their indifference in the face of death are proof of this; knowing beforehand that they will almost certainly not go unpunished their act is often an indirect suicide.

If we ask what the active anarchists wish to attain by their crimes the answer is principally that they wish to avenge upon society the misery experienced by others and by themselves; they wish to terrorize the ruling classes, in order to force upon them social reforms; they wish to set an example to the working classes and finally, they wish to satisfy their vanity, by making themselves talked of. Once committed, the crime is often the commencement of a vicious circle, since society avenges itself upon the author, who, in turn, is avenged by his friends; imitation thus leading to new crimes.

As in the case of all other crimes, I find for anarchism only social causes, and in the last analysis, only economic causes. To be sure, the individuals who commit these crimes are already predisposed in that direction, but this is true of other crimes also. Only the predisposition in these latter is simple, while that which leads to anarchistic crimes is much more complex. However, this predisposition alone explains nothing. I would ask those who think that only individual factors play any part, whether fanatical persons with all the characteristics of the anarchists of our time have not been found in all ages and countries. Everyone, I think, will answer in the affirmative. Well then, anarchistic crimes have occurred only during a certain period and in certain countries. No one can deny that there are as many persons predisposed to anarchistic crimes in a country like Germany, as there are in Italy, for example. Yet anarchistic crimes do not occur in Germany, for the good reason that the material conditions of the proletariat there are so much better than in Italy, and the degree of intellectual development in the working people is so much higher; the German working-man derides the "naïveté" of the anarchists, and detests their futile crimes. It is in the environment alone then that we find the causes of active anarchism, the poverty and ignorance in which the lower classes live.

VI
Pathological Crimes

So far we have been examining crime in its relation to the economic and social environment. We have not been able to discover the existence of individual factors; the celebrated formula, "crime = individual factor + social factor," has been shown to be incorrect if we are seeking for the causes of crime instead of asking why a certain individual has become a criminal. The conclusion obtained by sociology is the same as that arrived at in anthropology by authors like Manouvrier, Baer, and Näcke.

However, when one is trying to determine the cause of crime by sociology, certain cases are at times met with that cannot be explained in this way. For example, one person will steal useless objects which he is perfectly well able to buy; another will assault or kill without provocation, etc. These cases, it is true, are the exception, but they do exist and must not be neglected. We have here, then, real individual factors, factors which are found in certain individuals only. Other crimes, forming the great majority, are committed from motives which form the basis of all human acts, but are stronger with some few than they are with the general body of mankind. It is these individuals who run more danger than most of committing a crime when they live in a certain environment. The great mass of criminals differ only quantitatively from persons who never get into the courts; the criminals we are about to consider on the other hand differ qualitatively also.

One thing more before we ask ourselves what this individual factor is. As many authors have remarked, it very often happens that, even in the cases we are about to treat, there is a social factor. The proof of this is that individuals thus disposed to crime, but belonging to the well-to-do classes, seldom get to the point of committing them; because their education being better, the tendency is sooner noticed, they are better watched, and thus their committing a crime is often avoided. Born-criminals, in the sense of those who become criminals *whatever the circumstances may be* (the only meaning that can properly be given to the word "born" here), are doubtless very rare.

What, then, is the nature of this individual factor? It is especially the Italian school that has busied itself with this problem, and in doing so has rendered a service to science, although it has given an undue importance to this individual factor, attempting to discover it in all crimes. The first hypothesis given by Professor Lombroso was that of atavism, according to which the criminal was an individual in whom reappeared the characteristics of his remote ancestors, the desire to steal, kill, etc. It will not be far from the truth if we assert that almost no reputable scientist now accepts this hypothesis as correct. It has been attacked both from the side of sociology and from that of anthropology. Sociologists have proved that the facts contradict Professor Lombroso's thesis, for primitive peoples are neither thieves nor murderers, and our ancestors, consequently, may be regarded as cleared of the same charge.

Anthropologists also are strongly opposed to this hypothesis.

. . . Professor Jelgersma says that most of the anomalies observed in certain criminals have no atavistic character, such as unsymmetrical eyes and ears, abnormal growth of hair, etc. Dr. A. Baer makes the same remark . . . and goes on as follows: "The number of such abnormalities, which betray a disordered and an apparently genuine atavistic condition, is . . . so small and so accidental, that no force can be recognized in them that might serve for the explanation of criminality, or establish a causal connection with the criminal nature of an individual. Out of this mixture of stigmata of the most various origin and importance, to attempt to find the sole basis in their atavistic character is to do more than permissible violence to the facts."

After this beginning the Italian school put forth another explanation, to which it attached the more importance as the hypothesis of atavism fell into discredit: the criminal is either an epileptic or morally insane. Although the correctness of this hypothesis has not been proved any more than the other, the Italian school here found itself in a field recognized by criminal-anthropologists as its true one. At present one has even the right to say that the opinion in this regard is almost unanimous. *The origin of the tendencies of part of the criminals is to be found in the pathological nature of the individuals themselves.* These are disordered or degenerate, not, as some authors would have us believe, individuals differing more or less from the average, but persons who suffer from mental diseases, or whose nervous system is affected.

Among those disordered and degenerate, some individuals have tendencies not found in others (such as the desire to kill for the sake of killing), or their moral sentiments are excessively weak. It is to be noticed that we have met with degeneracy above, as it is to be named among the causes of alcoholism and prostitution also. In treating of economic crimes we saw that degenerates also run more danger than others of succumbing in the struggle for existence, and hence become criminals more easily. Thus we meet degeneracy both as a direct and as an indirect cause of crime.

We might leave the matter here, for we have come to a field other than that of sociology. However, one more question presents itself. To what extent are the economic system and its consequences the cause of these maladies? It is plain that this important question belongs in a work on sociology. We shall accordingly attempt to answer it briefly with the aid of competent authorities.

First of all, we note that heredity plays a great part in these maladies. The authors who have taken up the subject agree. It has been remarked that:

First, the inheritance of defects is not inevitable; degenerate parents may have sound children, though the chances are not very great.

Second, the disease of the parents is not always transmitted as such to the child, but the child may be predisposed to this same disease or one analogous. . . .

In speaking of heredity we come to the first relation between the diseases in question and the social environment, since, in our present society, human reproduction is intimately bound up with the economic life. A person who is diseased but rich is often in a position to marry and procreate, while he would have had a smaller chance if sexual selection alone had been effective. On the other hand, many well and strong individuals are prevented at present from establishing a family, since they lack the means to support it.

A second harmful kind of selection in our present society is found in the effect of militarism, which takes the strongest individuals, decimates them in time of war, or returns them to society weakened and diseased, while the weak have the greater chance to procreate.

In the third place, the ignorance of the harmful effects for humanity of the reproduction of degenerates is one of the principal reasons why degeneracy is so frequently present. This ignorance is great in the well-to-do classes, and naturally greater still among the poor. It is often repeated, and with truth, that man takes great care to improve his live stock by selection but takes none whatever in the matter of his own race; the weak and the diseased continue to reproduce themselves to the detriment of all society. The lack of all feeling of responsibility, natural to our intensely individualistic society, also contributes its share toward bringing to birth so many unhappy creatures for whom it would have been better if they had never existed.

If we ask how it happens that one individual or another is degenerate, we must answer that very often this degeneracy is due to heredity, either in part or altogether. But if we enquire into the causes of degeneracy in general heredity ceases to be a cause. As Professor Dallemagne says: "Heredity creates nothing; from heredity to heredity we must still go back to the cause."

What are at present the principal characteristics of the relation between degeneracy and the present economic system with its consequences? Some authors in treating of the etiology of degeneracy express themselves only in general terms, and point out no other cause than "unfavorable circumstances." Professor Jelgersma, for example, says: "The simple psychoses, melancholia, mania, etc. are caused by unfavorable circumstances. The cause of the psychoses of degeneracy is deeper; the unfavorable circumstances have exercised their influence from generation to generation, and thus an individual is born who is abnormal from birth."

These unfavorable circumstances must be more precisely defined, therefore. We shall divide them into four great groups.

First. *The material condition of the poor classes.* "To be well," says Dr. Toulouse, "one must be sufficiently fed, must clothe himself according to the season, be clean, not work beyond one's strength, and be more or less exempt from care." This is a simple truth of which all the world is convinced when it is a question of themselves or of their families, but which the physicians forget only too often when they are speaking of the social causes of diseases.

In the first place the poor classes are badly and insufficiently fed, and as a consequence grow weak, and the children born to them are inferior physically and mentally. The insufficient nourishment of the mother during her pregnancy, and the insufficient nourishment of the child during the first years of his life, are especially fatal to him. Then those who are badly fed are predisposed to tuberculosis, scrofula, and rickets, which, in their turn, may be the causes of degeneracy. Rickety women often have a contraction of the pelvis, which hinders child-birth, and may cause a lesion to the infant's brain. Note, for example, the opinion of Dr. Näcke, who says: "The social misery, bad hygiene and food . . . often enough beget a miserable generation and must already have injured the germ. The same causes, however, on the other hand easily produce feeble women with qualitatively and quantitatively insufficient milk, and most of all with a narrow pelvis, through which births take place with difficulty and to the detriment of the brain of the child. If now the above named factors come in later to affect the child, the derangement of nutrition will be further increased, and it is no wonder if all kinds of rickety and scrofulous symptoms appear in the body, and all kinds of children's ailments injure both body and mind."

In the second place, unsanitary dwellings and insufficient clothing are the cause of all sorts of diseases, especially tuberculosis, which in their turn may lead to degeneracy. The density of population in the great cities exercises its influence in the same direction.

In the third place, the long duration and intensity of the work forced upon the proletariat also contribute to degeneracy. For each individual there is a fixed measure of labor that he cannot pass without experiencing harmful consequences in body and mind. Dr. Lewy describes them as follows: "The consequences of immoderately long hours of labor are, a certain overexcitement of the nervous system which later gives place to a permanent debility, with which may be associated a dull headache as well as an inability to think clearly. If the overwork continues for a longer time, soon all the systems of the body are affected, the heart and larger arteries as well are injured in structure and function, disturbances of the regular circulation appear, manifested partly in swellings in various parts of the body, especially in the feet, and partly through hemorrhages. The brain ceases to function regularly, and so-called brain-symptoms appear, such as vertigo, ringing in the ears, deafness, defective vision, paralysis, and apoplexy. In the same way the liver, kidneys, and the digestive tract may be drawn into the general weakening process. The muscles become weak and slack, the body disposed to epidemic diseases, but especially prepared to vocational diseases, to which persons in a run-down condition most easily fall victim. If, then the end of the worker is not brought about prematurely by some intercurrent disease like typhus, under the immoderate strain he uses up his existing forces faster than he is in a position to replace them, and wastes away with tuberculosis of the lungs, so much the quicker, of course, the weaker he is constitutionally, and the younger he was when he had to submit to excessive labor."

The harmful consequences of long working hours make themselves felt especially in the trades which are already dangerous to health, like those where there is a great deal of dust produced, or those which use poisons like lead, mercury, etc. Monotony of work joined with long hours is also a cause of physical and intellectual deterioration. Professor Vogt says: "The less variety work presents, the more fatiguing is it, since it is only the same part of the muscles that are continually called upon, while the rest of the muscular system, in accordance with a well-known physiological law, degenerates from misuse and wastes away.

To a still higher degree the uniformity of work has a deteriorating effect upon the mental powers; these become weakened much more quickly in the case of long continued fatigue than the muscles, while the unexercised mental faculties at the same time become stunted."

The present economic system has also led to the work of women and children, and consequently to an important cause of the degeneration of the race. The number of women forced to take part in trades for which they are ill-fitted by nature is very great. The fear of being discharged, and the impossibility of doing without their wages make women with child continue to work up to the last moment of their pregnancy, and recommence shortly after childbirth, leading to very harmful results both for them and for their children. Then child labor prevents the normal development of the children and ages them prematurely.

Further, the cares and restlessness consequent upon the uncertainty of life may be causes of the weakening of the nervous system and the origin of a neurosis.

Finally, when an individual of this class falls sick his restoration to health may be hindered by the lack of care and medical assistance and the necessity of recommencing work too soon.

Second. *The condition of the well-to-do classes.* Most of the causes producing degeneracy in the poor classes do not appear among the well-to-do. With the latter there can be no question of insufficient food or clothing, or of bad housing. Yet in the well-to-do classes the idle, from their manner of living and this lack of regular exercise, are led to excesses of all kinds, which may make them too, in another way, subject to degeneracy.

In the active part of the bourgeoisie, among the manufacturers, merchants, etc., the case is different. They are constantly absorbed in the question of how to increase their wealth, or, if they are unfortunate, they live in fear of losing the position gained. They are in a state of agitation, of permanent overexcitement. So there are numbers in the bourgeois class who overtax their minds, with the resulting chance of neurasthenia, even where the individual is not predisposed to it. All this applies also to the liberal professions, though in a smaller degree; there also the great competition has harmful consequences for the nerves. In "La famille névropathique" Dr. Féré thus describes the consequences of overdriving: ". . . excessive cerebral labor, intellectual and, still more, moral overwork, the continual pre-occupations of the struggle for existence are conditions eminently fit to bring on functional troubles in the nervous system. Neurasthenia, like hysteria, may be considered as a chronic fatigue. The fatigue, to be sure, gives place to a number of troubles peculiar to neurasthenia. And these troubles, even if only temporary, cannot fail to have the most harmful effect upon children conceived under these conditions."

The opinion of the celebrated alienist Maudsley is also very interesting; he says: "Perhaps one, and certainly not the least, of the ill effects which spring from some of the conditions of our present civilization, is seen in the general dread and disdain of poverty, in the eager passion to become rich. The practical gospel of the age, testified everywhere by faith and works, is that of money-getting; men are estimated mainly by the amount of their wealth, take social rank accordingly, and consequently bend all their energies to acquire that which gains them esteem and influence. The result is that in the higher departments of trade and commerce speculations of all sorts are eagerly entered in, and that many people are kept in a continued state of excitement and anxiety by the fluctuations of the money market. In the lower branches of trade there is the same eager desire for petty gains; and the continued absorption of the mind in these small acquisitions generates a littleness of mind and meanness of spirit, where it does not lead to actual dishonesty, which are nowhere displayed in a more pitiable form than by certain petty tradesmen. The occupation which a man is entirely engaged in does not fail to modify his character, and the reaction upon the individual's nature of a life which is being spent with the sole aim of becoming rich, is most baneful. It is not that the fluctuations of excitement unhinge the merchant's mind and lead to maniacal outbreaks, although that does sometimes happen; it is not that failure in the paroxysm of some crisis prostrates his energies and makes him melancholic, although that also is occasionally witnessed; but it is that exclusiveness of his life-aim and occupation too often saps the moral or altruistic element in his nature, makes him become egoistic, formal, and unsympathetic, and in his person deteriorates the nature of humanity. What is the consequence? If one conviction has been fixed in my mind more distinctly than another by observation of instances, it is that it is extremely unlikely such a man will beget healthy children; on the contrary, it is extremely likely that the deterioration of nature which he has acquired will be transmitted as an evil heritage to his children. In several instances in which the father has toiled upwards from poverty to vast wealth, with the aim and hope of founding a family, I have witnessed the results in a degeneracy, mental and physical, of his offspring, which has sometimes gone as far as extinction of the family in the third or fourth generation. When the evil is not so extreme as madness or ruinous vice, the savour of a mother's influence having been present, it may still be manifest in an instinctive cunning and duplicity, and an extreme selfishness of nature—a nature not having the capacity of a true moral conception or altruistic feeling. Whatever opinion other more experienced observers may hold, I cannot but think, after what I have seen, that the extreme passion for getting rich, absorbing the whole energies of life, does predispose to mental degeneration in the offspring—either to moral defect, or to moral and intellectual deficiency, or to outbreaks of positive insanity under the conditions of life."

We could cite a number of other competent authorities to

prove that the present economic system exacts from those who direct production also, intellectual efforts such as the nervous system cannot endure indefinitely.

Third. *Syphilis.* Aside from the fact that this malady is very probably the cause of general paralysis, it takes its place among the important factors of degeneracy to this extent, that the children of syphilitics are often degenerates. This fact being generally recognized we shall not dwell on it.

*   *   *

This would not be the time to speak of syphilis as a cause of degeneracy, if the extension of this malady were not intimately bound up with prostitution, which is, in its turn, determined by the economic environment. Dr. Blaschko says of it: "The principal source of venereal infection of course is, and remains sexual intercourse outside of wedlock, especially prostitution."

As a social cause of the great extension of syphilis it is well to point out the profound ignorance of the extent and the danger of venereal diseases, to which less attention is paid than to others (hospitals not receiving patients affected by them, relief funds not aiding those having syphilis, etc.). Like other diseases these have the most harmful consequences for those who live under bad conditions.

Fourth. *Alcoholism.* Alcoholism undoubtedly belongs to the very important causes of degeneracy. There are few questions upon which competent authors are as unanimous as they are upon this. There is a wealth of material for quotation but we will limit ourselves to the words of Professor Dallemagne, who, after quoting the opinion of such authorities as Moral, Magnan, and others concludes by saying: "Alcohol is an essential factor of degeneracy. It can by itself create all the degenerate and unbalanced states, and this question appears definitely decided." Dr. Legrain gives the following figures upon the consequences

of chronic alcoholism of the parents upon the children. Out of
215 families of alcoholics in four generations (814 individuals),
there were found: 42% of alcoholics, 60.9% of degenerates,
13.9% morally insane, 22.7% had had convulsions, 20% were
hysterical or epileptic, and 19% were insane. These are striking
figures, and banish all doubt of the harmful influence of
alcohol!

It must still further be observed, that the very frequent adulteration of alcohol leads to especially harmful consequences:
and that alcohol exerts an especially harmful effect upon the
ill-nourished.

We have come now to the end of our remarks upon the social
and economic causes of degeneracy. Although they are plainly
not the only ones, yet it is certain that their part in the etiology
of degeneracy is very important, and even preponderating

VII
Conclusions

What are the conclusions to be drawn from what has gone before? When we sum up the results that we have obtained it becomes plain that economic conditions occupy a much more important place in the etiology of crime than most authors have given them.

First we have seen that the present economic system and its consequences weaken the social feelings. The basis of the economic system of our day being exchange, the economic interests of men are necessarily found to be in opposition. This is a trait that capitalism has in common with other modes of production. But its principal characteristic is that the means of production are in the hands of a few, and most men are altogether deprived of them. Consequently, persons who do not possess the means of production are forced to sell their labor to those who do, and these, in consequence of their economic preponderance, force them to make the exchange for the mere necessaries of life, and to work as much as their strength permits.

This state of things especially stifles men's social instincts; it develops, on the part of those with power, the spirit of domination, and of insensibility to the ills of others, while it awakens jealousy and servility on the part of those who depend upon them. Further the contrary interests of those who have property, and the idle and luxurious life of some of them, also contribute to the weakening of the social instincts.

The material condition, and consequently the intellectual condition, of the proletariat are also a reason why the moral plane of that class is not high. The work of children brings them into contact with persons to associate with whom is fatal to their morals. Long working hours and monotonous labor brutalize those who are forced into them; bad housing conditions contribute also to debase the moral sense, as do the uncertainty of existence, and finally absolute poverty, the frequent consequence of sickness and unemployment. Ignorance and lack of training of any kind also contribute their quota. Most demoralizing of all is the status of the lower proletariat.

The economic position of woman contributes also to the weakening of the social instincts.

The present organization of the family has great importance as regards criminality. It charges the legitimate parents with the care of the education of the child; the community concerns itself with the matter very little. It follows that a great number of children are brought up by persons who are totally incapable of doing it properly. As regards the children of the proletariat, there can be no question of the education properly so called, on account of the lack of means and the forced absence of one or both of the parents. The school tends to remedy this state of things, but the results do not go far enough. The harmful consequences of the present organization of the family make themselves felt especially in the case of the children of the lower proletariat, orphans, and illegitimate children. For these the community does but little, though their need of adequate help is the greatest.

Prostitution, alcoholism, and militarism, which result, in the last analysis, from the present social order, are phenomena that have demoralizing consequences.

As to the different kinds of crime, we have shown that the very important group of economic criminality finds its origin on the one side in the absolute poverty and the cupidity brought about by the present economic environment, and on the other in the moral abandonment and bad education of the children of the poorer classes. Then, professional criminals are principally recruited from the class of occasional criminals, who, finding themselves rejected everywhere after their liberation, fall lower and lower. The last group of economic crimes (fraudulent bankruptcy, etc.) is so intimately connected with our present mode of production, that it would not be possible to commit it under another.

The relation between sexual crimes and economic conditions is less direct; nevertheless these also give evidence of the decisive influence of these conditions. We have called attention to the four following points.

First, there is a direct connection between the crime of adultery and the present organization of society, which requires that the legal dissolution of a marriage should be impossible or very difficult.

Second, sexual crimes upon adults are committed especially by unmarried men; and since the number of marriages depends in its turn upon the economic situation, the connection is clear; and those who commit these crimes are further almost exclusively illiterate, coarse, raised in an environment almost without sexual morality, and regard the sexual life from the wholly animal side.

Third, the causes of sexual crime upon children are partly the same as those of which we have been speaking, with the addition of prostitution.

Fourth, alcoholism greatly encourages sexual assaults.

As to the relation between crimes of vengeance and the present constitution of society, we have noted that it produces conflicts without number; statistics have shown that those who commit them are almost without exception poor and uncivilized, and that alcoholism is among the most important causes of these crimes.

Infanticide is caused in part by poverty, and in part by the opprobrium incurred by the unmarried mother (an opprobrium resulting from the social utility of marriage).

Political criminality comes solely from the economic system and its consequences.

Finally, economic and social conditions are also important factors in the etiology of degeneracy, which is in its turn a cause of crime.

Upon the basis of what has gone before, we have a right to say that the part played by economic conditions in criminality is preponderant, even decisive.

This conclusion is of the highest importance for the prevention of crime. If it were principally the consequence of innate human qualities (atavism, for example), the pessimistic conclusion that crime is a phenomenon inseparably bound up with the social life would be well founded. But the facts show that it is rather the optimistic conclusion that we must draw, that where crime is the consequence of economic and social conditions, we can combat it by changing those conditions.

However important crime may be as a social phenomenon, however terrible may be the injuries and the evil that it brings upon humanity, the development of society will not depend upon the question as to what are the conditions which could restrain crime or make it disappear, if possible; the evolution of society will proceed independently of this question.

What is the direction that society will take under these continual modifications? This is not the place to treat fully of this subject. In my opinion the facts indicate quite clearly what the direction will be. The productivity of labor has increased to an unheard of degree, and will assuredly increase in the future. The concentration of the means of production into the hands of a few progresses continually; in many branches it has reached such a degree that the fundamental principle of the present economic system, competition, is excluded, and has been replaced by monopoly. On the other hand the working class is becoming more and more organized, and the opinion is very generally held among working-men that the causes of material and intellectual poverty can be eliminated only by having the means of production held in common.

Supposing that this were actually realized, what would be the consequences as regards criminality? Let us take up this question for a moment. Although we can give only personal opinions as to the details of such a society, the general outlines can be traced with certainty.

The chief difference between a society based upon the community of the means of production and our own is that material poverty would be no longer known. Thus one great part of economic criminality (as also one part of infanticide) would be rendered impossible, and one of the greatest demoralizing forces of our present society would be eliminated. And then, in this way those social phenomena so productive of crime, prostitution and alcoholism, would lose one of their principal factors. Child labor and overdriving would no longer take place, and bad housing, the source of much physical and moral evil, would no longer exist.

With material poverty there would disappear also that intellectual poverty which weighs so heavily upon the proletariat; culture would no longer be the privilege of some, but a possession common to all. The consequences of this upon criminality would be very important, for we have seen that even in our present society with its numerous conflicts, the members of the propertied classes, who have often but a veneer of civilization, are almost never guilty of crimes of vengeance. There is the more reason to admit that in a society where interests were not opposed, and where civilization was universal, these crimes would be no longer present, especially since alcoholism also proceeds in large part from the intellectual poverty of the poorer classes. And what is true of crimes of vengeance, is equally true of sexual crimes in so far as they have the same etiology.

A large part of the economic criminality (and also prostitution to a certain extent) has its origin in the cupidity excited by the present economic environment. In a society based upon the community of the means of production, great contrasts of fortune would, like commercial capital, be lacking, and thus cupidity would find no food. These crimes will not totally disappear so long as there has not been a redistribution of property according to the maxim, "to each according to his needs," something that will probably be realized, but not in the immediate future.

The changes in the position of woman which are taking place in our present society, will lead, under this future mode of production, to her economic independence, and consequently to her social independence as well. It is accordingly probable that the criminality of woman will increase in comparison with that of man during the transition period. But the final result will be the disappearance of the harmful effects of the economic and social preponderance of man.

As to the education of children under these new conditions it is difficult to be definite. However, it is certain that the community will concern itself seriously with their welfare. It will see to it that the children whose parents cannot or will not be responsible for them, are well cared for. By acting in this way it will remove one of the most important causes of crime. There is no doubt that the community will exercise also a strict control over the education of children; it cannot be affirmed, however, that the time will come when the children of a number of parents will be brought up together by capable persons; this will depend principally upon the intensity that the social sentiments may attain.

As soon as the interests of all are no longer opposed to each other, as they are in our present society, there will no longer be a question either of politics ("a fortiori" of political *crimes*) or of militarism.

Such a society will not only remove the causes which now make men egoistic, but will awaken, on the contrary, a strong feeling of altruism. We have seen that this was already the case with the primitive peoples, where their economic interests were not in opposition. In a larger measure this will be realized under a mode of production in common, the interests of all being the same.

In such a society there can be no question of crime properly so called. The eminent criminologist, Manouvrier, in treating of the prevention of crime expresses himself thus: "The maxim to apply is, act so that every man shall always have more interest in being useful to his fellows than in harming them." It is precisely in a society where the community of the means of production has been realized that this maxim will obtain its complete application. There will be crimes committed by pathological individuals, but this will come rather within the sphere of the physician than that of the judge. And then we may even reach a state where these cases will decrease in large measure, since the social causes of degeneracy will disappear, and procreation by degenerates be checked through the increased knowledge of the laws of heredity and the increasing sense of moral responsibility.

"It is society that prepares the crime," says the true adage of Quetelet. For all those who have reached this conclusion, and are not insensible to the sufferings of humanity, this statement is sad, but contains a ground of hope. It is sad, because society punishes severely those who commit the crime which she has herself prepared. It contains a ground of hope, since it promises to humanity the possibility of some day delivering itself from one of its most terrible scourges.